THE ORGANIZATION OF ISLAMIC COOPERATION'S JIHAD ON FREE SPEECH

By Deborah Weiss, Esq.

CIVILIZATION JIHAD READER SERIES

Volume 3

ISBN-13: 978-1511960595

ISBN-10: 1511960590

Library of Congress Control Number: 2015906998

CreateSpace Independent Publishing Platform, North Charleston, SC

Copyright © 2015, by Deborah Weiss, Esq. All rights reserved.

The Organization of Islamic Cooperation's Jihad on Free Speech
is published in the United States by the Center for Security Policy Press,
a division of the Center for Security Policy.

June 6, 2015

The information contained in this monograph may be distributed for personal non-professional and non-commercial use. Reproduction or distribution for professional or commercial purposes without written permission from the author constitutes a copyright violation.

THE CENTER FOR SECURITY POLICY
1901 Pennsylvania Avenue, Suite 201 Washington, DC 20006
Phone: (202) 835-9077 | Email: info@securefreedom.org
For more information, please see securefreedom.org

Book design by Adam Savit
Cover design by Alex VanNess

ABOUT THE AUTHOR

Deborah Weiss, Esq. is a contributing author to the book, "Saudi Arabia and the Global Islamic Terrorist Network" and is the primary writer and researcher for the book, "Council on American-Islamic Relations: Its Use of Lawfare and Intimidation". Considered an expert in the Islamist stifling of free speech, her speeches and articles can be found on www.vigilancenow.org

CONTENTS

ABOUT THE AUTHOR 3

CONTENTS 5

FOREWORD 7

INTRODUCTION 11

WHAT IS THE ORGANIZATION OF ISLAMIC COOPERATION (OIC)? 13

THE OIC's CHARTER 15

THE OIC'S MISSION 16

COMBATING DEFAMATION OF RELIGIONS 18

LEGAL STATUS OF UNITED NATIONS RESOLUTIONS 21

TIME LINE 22

THE OIC'S EXAMPLES OF "ISLAMOPHOBIA" 24

THE UN HUMAN RIGHTS COUNCIL PASSES A RULE 25

STATE DEPARTMENT REQUEST 26

RESOLUTION 16/18: TO COMBAT INTOLERANCE BASED
ON RELIGION OR BELIEF 27

THE OIC'S USE OF PRE-EXISTING LEGAL INSTRUMENTS 30

THE DEFINITION OF ISLAMOPHOBIA 33

SECRETARY CLINTON'S ANNOUNCEMENT OF THE ISTANBUL PROCESS 35

THE US STATE DEPARTMENT ISTANBUL CONFERENCE 36

THE PROCESS OF LOSING FREEDOM OF SPEECH 38

ADDITIONAL ANALYSIS 40

REAL LIFE CONSEQUENCES OF PUTTING INTO EFFECT THE COMBATING DEFAMATION OF RELIGIONS CONCEPT 43

THE OBAMA ADMINISTRATION'S PURPOSEFUL DENIAL OF ALL THINGS ISLAM 46

WHAT AMERICA SHOULD BE DOING 48

AFTERWORD 51

APPENDIX 1: TEXT OF UNHRC RESOLUTION 10/22 55

APPENDIX 2: TEXT OF UN RESOLUTION 16/18 62

FOREWORD

Thanks to the tremendous wisdom of our Founding Fathers, we Americans enjoy the precious rights enshrined in the Constitution and Bill of Rights. Among these, the latter's guarantee of freedom of speech must count as one of the most important bulwarks for a free people against tyranny ever enshrined in any legal system in the history of mankind. Few other legal systems even come close to granting – and defending – the kinds of protections for free speech and expression too often taken for granted in the United States.

At the polar opposite end of the tyranny-liberty spectrum are the tenets of the Islamic supremacist legal-politico-military code its adherents call shariah. They are designed, not to champion individual freedoms, but rather to enforce the dictates of Islam's totalitarian shariah doctrine over all, Muslims and non-Muslims alike. It is hardly surprising, therefore, that proponents of shariah would seek, as a top priority, to severely curtail – if not *abolish outright* – freedom of speech.

The most prominent of such Islamic supremacists is the Organization of Islamic Cooperation (OIC), comprised at the head-of-state level of representatives from 56 Muslim countries, plus the Palestinian Authority. As the second-largest multinational organization in the world (after only the United Nations itself), the OIC claims to represent some 1.6 billion Muslims across the globe in ways that lead some to call the organization a proto-Caliphate.

As this volume – the third in the Secure Freedom (Center for Security Policy) Civilization Jihad Reader Series – makes clear, thanks to the petrodollar wealth of a number of the OIC's members and their willingness to act as a bloc in furtherance of a shared agenda, the organization enjoys disproportionate influence at the United Nations.

For example, twenty-five years ago, the OIC nations acted in concert to up-end one of the UN's foundational principles: the body's at-least-rhetorical commitment to fundamental freedoms enshrined in the Universal Charter of Human Rights. The OIC members formally withdrew from compliance with the Charter's guarantees after adopting in 1990 an alternative called the Cairo Declaration, which asserts that the only human rights Muslims recognize are those granted under shariah.

Freedom of expression is not one of the liberties shariah countenances. To the contrary, as was recently vividly showcased in Garland, Texas on May 3, 2015, shariah-adherent Muslims believe it is their duty to punish severely – including with murder – any who violate their doctrine's injunctions against blasphemy, or otherwise give offense to the faithful.

Recognizing the critical role that freedom of expression plays in the preservation of a free society, and realizing the deadly threat posed by shariah's liberty-crushing mandates, author, essayist and attorney Deborah Weiss has become one of the nation's top experts on the OIC and its agenda to curtail so-called "defamation of religions." With this new monograph on *The OIC's Jihad on Free Speech*, Ms. Weiss brings her formidable expertise – honed over the years since she survived the 9/11 attacks in New York – and her meticulous research to bear on a critical challenge of our time: Will the United States, like other Western societies, submit to the Islamic supremacists' campaign to impose their shariah-restricted speech codes worldwide?

Ms. Weiss illuminates the stranglehold that the OIC voting-bloc at the United Nations holds over the organization's notorious Human Rights Council (UNHRC). She shows how – with considerable help from President Obama and others in or influential with his administration – the UNHRC has served as a vehicle for insisting that non-Muslim nations adopt in their own lands what amount to statutes criminalizing expression that gives offense to Muslims.

Ms. Weiss' account of the leading role in this campaign to limit Americans' free speech rights played by then-Secretary of State Hillary Clinton and the U.S. Department of State is particularly troubling. We learn that Mrs. Clinton collaborated closely with the man who was at the time the Secretary General of the Organization of Islamic Cooperation, Ekmeleddin Ihsanoglu, through a series of high-level meetings that came to be known as "The Istanbul Process." Its explicit purpose was to find ways to accommodate the OIC's demands for the official stifling of any critical examination of Islam.

The Obama administration and the OIC, together with the European Union, succeeded in securing the adoption of UNHRC Resolution 16/18, a measure that would make it unlawful to engage in speech that incites "discrimination" or "hostility" toward "religions".

The OIC applies, moreover, a "consequence-based test" for "offensive" speech that places all responsibility for potentially violent responses on the speaker, while absolving of any responsibility for their actions Muslim individuals who might retaliate violently. Here again, Ms. Weiss points out the troubling willingness of Secretary Clinton to lend the authority of the U.S. government to such efforts, even to the extent that she told an OIC gathering in 2011 that it was time to use "some old-fashioned techniques of peer pressure and shaming" to shut down criticism of Islam.

The assault against the First Amendment here and expression elsewhere has also benefitted from the relentless promotion of the term "Islamophobia." Deborah Weiss explains that this purported condition was first introduced at an OIC summit held in Mecca, Saudi Arabia in 2006. The organization's Ten-Year "Program of Action" adopted at that event identified "combating Islamophobia" as one of its top goals.

At a subsequent summit in 2008, the OIC unveiled its 1st Annual OIC Observatory Report on Islamophobia, a document now issued yearly (along with monthly "bulletins"). These products are comprised largely of media reports and private sector and official documentation of jihadist and other shariah-compliant activity. Even truthful accounts about Islamic teachings and practices and behavior pursuant thereto are condemned as offensive and Islamophobic. That senior officials of the U.S. government, who have all sworn to "protect and defend the Constitution," could contribute in any way to the advance of this agenda is appalling and extremely ominous for our Republic.

In short, as Deborah Weiss demonstrates powerfully, the need to defend free speech has never been greater. As she correctly observes, "Freedom is not the normal state of the world. It is the exception." It will take the concerted effort of every patriotic American to counter the OIC's assault on our Constitution, especially given the help it is receiving from well-funded Islamists and their enablers in this country.

Secure Freedom is proud to present this superb addition to its Civilization Jihad Reader Series with the encouragement that the reader take to heart its warnings of a particularly insidious assault on our liberty – and heed Deborah Weiss' clarion call to join forces to resist it. This is a moment for citizens, legislators and policymakers alike to respond with determination to defend this country's founding principles. That effort should include an end to all cooperation with the Islamic supremacists of the Organization of Islamic Cooperation, including the Istanbul Process. It should also entail a vigorous and unapologetic commitment to freedom of expression and its employment as an indispensable weapon in the execution of a comprehensive strategy to defeat the Global Jihad Movement.

Frank J. Gaffney, Jr.
President and CEO
Secure Freedom

INTRODUCTION

Freedom of speech is a fundamental human right and a foundational freedom from which all other freedoms flow.[1] Tyrants throughout history have always known that book-burning and censorship are useful tools toward the acquisition of power and the oppression of dissent.[2]

Information is power and censorship is designed to suppress the free flow of information: both its dissemination and its receipt. In extreme cases, censorship goes even further, serving as a thought-stopping measure. Indeed, words represent ideas. Thus, the fewer words in a given lexicon, the fewer ideas can be had.[3]

We are in a war. It is not a war on terror, for terrorism is merely a tactic. We are in a war of ideas: it is freedom versus tyranny; liberty versus shariah. French Emperor Napoleon Bonaparte stated that "[T]here are but two powers in the world, the sword and the mind. In the long run the sword is always beaten by the mind."[4] Islamists know they cannot win a military war against the West or the US in particular. But they also know what we don't: that with a purpose, a plan and persistence, the battle for hearts and minds in the war of ideas is winnable. We ignore this critical aspect of war at our own peril.

---

[1] See http://eclj.org/pdf/eclj_draftgeneralcommentno34-article19_20110201.pdf page 6, accessed March 3, 2015.
[2] http://www.beaconforfreedom.org/liste.html?tid=415&art_id=475, accessed December 22, 2014.
[3] George Orwell, "The Principles of Newspeak", Appendix to "1984", http://www.newspeakdictionary.com/ns-prin.html, accessed December 22, 2014.
[4] http://www.goodreads.com/author/quotes/210910.Napoleon, accessed November 23, 2014.

WHAT IS THE ORGANIZATION OF ISLAMIC COOPERATION (OIC)?

After the fall of the Ottoman Empire, there were numerous conferences in the Middle East contemplating the creation of an intergovernmental organization to determine what entity would succeed the Caliphate and represent the Islamic Ummah.[5]

However, the alleged "Zionist arson attack against the Al-Aqsa Mosque on August 21, 1969" in "occupied Jerusalem" constituted the last straw for Muslim countries that viewed themselves as defeated. Despite the fact that the attack was not committed by a Jew,[6] this incident gave rise to the formation of the OIC.

The Organization of Islamic Cooperation (OIC) is the second largest international organization in the world, behind only the United Nations. It is the largest Islamic organization in the world, claiming to represent 1.5 billion Muslims around the world. It is comprised of 56 UN Member States plus the Palestinian Authority.*[7] Some experts liken the OIC to the pre-cursor of a future potential Islamic Caliphate.[8]

Saudi Arabia plays an important role in the OIC. The OIC is based in Jeddah, Saudi Arabia which indeed is its largest financial backer. As such, Saudi Arabia constitutes its most influential state. It largely determines, along with a handful of other financial donors, what direction the OIC will take, which issues it will address, and the position it takes on those issues. Pakistan, Iran and Turkey constitute some of the other powerful states within the OIC.[9] In January of 2014,

---

[5] http://www.icnl.org/research/monitor/oic.html, accessed November 8, 2014.

[6] http://www.oicun.org/2/23/, accessed November 8, 2014. See also http://usa.mediamonitors.net/Headlines/Organization-of-Islamic-Conference-Vision-for-2050 accessed November 8, 2014. The so-called "Zionist attack" is the standard Arab story line, despite the fact that the arsonist turned out to be an Australian Christian who was promptly arrested and tried by the Israeli government. At trial, he was found to be insane and accordingly was hospitalized in a mental institution.
http://www.takeapen.org/Takeapen/Templates/showpage.asp?DBID=1&LNGID=1&TMID=84&FID=631, accessed December 22, 2014.

[7] http://www.oicun.org/2/23/, accessed December 22, 2014. At the time of this writing, technically there are 55 UN Member States in the OIC and the Palestinian Authority, as Syria is on suspension. http://www.jpost.com/Middle-East/OIC-suspends-Syria-over-violence-against-rebels, accessed December 22, 2014.

[8] See http://www.americanthinker.com/articles/2010/09/oic_and_the_modern_caliphate.html, accessed December 22, 2014.

[9] http://www.cfr.org/religion/organization-islamic-conference/p22563, accessed December 22, 2014.

Iyad bin Amin Madani, the former Saudi Minister of Culture and Information became the OIC's new Secretary General, replacing former Secretary General, Ekmeleddin Ihsanoglu, from Turkey. [10]

The OIC Member States vote together as a bloc in the UN, which affords them substantial power as the UN only has a total of 193 Member States. Indeed, the OIC has a stranglehold on the UN Human Rights Council (HRC) and arguably constitutes the most influential power in the United Nations as a whole. Yet, most people have never heard of it.

Previously called "The Organization of Islamic Conference", the OIC changed its name in June of 2011, in what appears to be a public relations move. It is now called "The Organization of Islamic Cooperation",[11] but its goals remain identical to what they were previously.

---

[10] http://www.arabnews.com/news/502216?page=3&quicktabs_stat2=0, accessed December 22, 2014.
[11] http://www.taqrib.info/english/index.php?option=com_content&view=article&id=365:change-of-oic-logo-and-name-to-organisation-of-the-islamic-cooperation&catid=41:2009-08-31-05-03-32&Itemid=69, accessed December 22, 2014.

THE OIC'S CHARTER

The OIC's Charter asserts that its mission is to promote Islamic values, to revitalize Islam's pioneering role in the world, to strengthen solidarity among Muslim States, to unify the Muslim voice, to support the "Palestinian struggle", to defend Member State sovereignty, to assist Muslim communities outside the jurisdiction of Member States, to present a single position on the international stage in matters of common interest, to defend the "true image of Islam, and to combat "defamation of Islam." [12]

The OIC's charter also claims to promote "peace, compassion, tolerance, equality, justice and human dignity" as well as to fight terrorism.[13] However, as this monograph will explain, these concepts are viewed through the extraordinarily skewed lens of shariah (Islamic law) and a redefinition of words. Thus, the OIC's positions and actions run contrary to its claims.

---

[12] http://www.oic-oci.org/oicv2/page/?p_id=53&p_ref=27&lan=en, accessed November 8, 2014.
[13] Id.

THE OIC'S MISSION

Despite the fact that the OIC claims to be a proponent of human rights, its understanding of human rights is expressly limited to that which is permitted by shariah.[14] The OIC holds itself out as a moderate organization. However, it is an Islamist supremacist organization whose long term vision is the implementation of shariah on a world wide scale, to which both Muslims and non-Muslims would have to submit.

The OIC mouths lip service to human rights, but fails to support the UN Declaration of Human Rights. Instead, it has proffered an alternative document, titled "the Cairo Declaration on Human Rights in Islam."[15] Many of its prominent nation states believe that the UN Declaration of Human Rights fails to take into account the "cultural and religious context of Islamic countries". Indeed, Iran views it as a "secular interpretation of a Judeo – Christian tradition which can't be implemented without trespassing on Islamic law". The Cairo Declaration, which is not the subject of this monograph, in short, limits all "human rights" to those permitted by shariah. It treats Muslims as superior to non-Muslims, men as superior to women, severely restricts freedom of expression and freedom of religion, and allows the right to life and freedom from government-inflicted bodily harm only to the extent permissible by shariah.[16] The Cairo Declaration is relevant to the OIC's UN resolutions because a proper analysis will view all ideas set forth by the OIC through the lens of shariah, with its concordant limiting language.

In furtherance of its long term goals, in the more immediate term, the OIC seeks to internationally outlaw, and ultimately criminalize all criticism of Sharia, Islam, Islamic theocracies, Muslims, and even Islamic terrorism.[17]

Though the OIC claims that it supports freedom of speech, it also insists that freedom of speech does not include freedom to make blasphemous comments or "insults to Islam".[18] Indeed, its support for the concept of combating defamation of religions serves to justify the harsh blasphemy laws that already exist in OIC countries

---

[14] http://www.americanthinker.com/articles/2008/12/human_rights_vs_islamic_rights.html, accessed February 15, 2015.
[15] http://www1.umn.edu/humanrts/instree/cairodeclaration.html, accessed December 22, 2014.
[16] http://www.americanthinker.com/articles/2008/12/human_rights_vs_islamic_rights.html, accessed December 22, 2014.
[17] http://www.gatestoneinstitute.org/3474/blasphemy-laws-europe, accessed January 2, 2015.
[18] http://articles.chicagotribune.com/2012-09-19/news/sns-rt-us-protests-religions-blasphemybre88i1eg-20120919_1_blasphemy-law-muslim-cleric-ekmeleddin-ihsanoglu, accessed December 22, 2014.

like Sudan, Saudi Arabia, Iran, Pakistan and Egypt.[19] In fact, all Muslim majority countries already have some sort of Islamic blasphemy codes, whether formal or informal.[20]

It is clear that the defamation of religions campaign is targeted toward the West to achieve the equivalent of Islamic blasphemy laws.[21] Were the OIC to openly demand the implementation of Islamic blasphemy laws in Western countries, the Free World would turn a deaf ear.[22] Therefore, the OIC uses multi-lateral conferences, "consensus building" and legal instruments such as UN resolutions, with language more palatable to free societies, in order to achieve its goals gradually and incrementally.

Under the guise of responsible speech, sensitive speech or politically correct speech, the OIC's true goal is to stifle the West's freedom of speech.[23] And unfortunately, it is making headway.

---

[19] See http://www.harvard-jlpp.com/wp-content/uploads/2013/10/LeoFinal.pdf page 1, accessed January 2, 2015.
[20] See http://www.humanrightsfirst.org/sites/default/files/Compendium-Blasphemy-Laws.pdf accessed January 2, 2015. See also http://www.humanrightsfirst.org/sites/default/files/Compendium-Related-to-Blasphemy-Laws.pdf, accessed January 2, 2015.
[21] See http://www.gatestoneinstitute.org/3474/blasphemy-laws-europe, accessed March 3, 2015. See also https://thejihadproject.files.wordpress.com/2012/02/001_islamphobia_rep_may_07_08.pdf pages 1-10, accessed January 2, 2015.
[22] See http://www.reuters.com/article/2012/10/15/us-islam-blasphemy-idUSBRE89E18U20121015, accessed February 15, 2015.
[23] See, e.g., http://www.todayszaman.com/op-ed_freedom-of-expression-is-not-a-license-to-incite-hatred-and-intolerance-1-by-ekmeleddin-ihsanoglu-_289645.html, accessed February 15, 2015.

COMBATING DEFAMATION OF RELIGIONS

The first UN resolution to be discussed here, is titled "Combating Defamation of Religions". [24]

The concept of combating defamation of religions (herein referred to as "defamation of religions") takes an idea, or a religion and provides it with legal protection from criticism.[25] However, in the American legal system, only people can be defamed.[26] Ideas, policies and religions are not subject to defamation laws. Additionally, in the American legal system, defamation consists of an intentionally false statement of fact. Truth is a defense. If one says something bad about a person and it's a true statement of fact, it is not considered defamatory. Additionally, mere opinion as opposed to fact is always considered constitutionally protected speech.[27]

By stark contrast, the OIC's definition of defamation of Islam includes anything that sheds a negative light on Islam or Muslims, even if it is true and even if it is mere opinion. Additionally, it goes even further by including anything that violates Islamic blasphemy laws. For example, drawing a picture of the Muslim Prophet Muhammad is blasphemy in Islam even if he is shown in a positive light.[28] The OIC would consider this defamation as well.

Thus, the OIC's use of the word "defamation" is tantamount to the word "blasphemy", and more specifically Islamic blasphemy, not that of Christianity or any other religion.[29]

Indeed, the original draft of the OIC's resolution was titled, "Combating Defamation of Islam", but when it failed to get sufficient support, the OIC amended the title to "Combating Defamation of Religions". Yet, the text of this resolution

---

[24] This "Combatting Defamation of Religions" resolution, with minor variations, is the same resolution introduced into the Commission on Human Rights in 1999 and thereafter, and in the General Assembly in 2005 and thereafter, and in the Human Rights Council 2006 and thereafter. See, e.g., UN HRC Resolution 10/22 adopted March 26, 2009: http://ap.ohchr.org/documents/E/HRC/resolutions/A_HRC_RES_10_22.pdf accessed February, 15, 2014.
[25] See http://www.uscirf.gov/sites/default/files/resources/stories/PDFs/PolicyFocus_USCIRF_final.pdf pages 1-2, accessed February 15, 2015.
[26] Id at page 2.
[27] See http://www.nolo.com/legal-encyclopedia/defamation-law-made-simple-29718.html, accessed January 2, 2014.
[28] http://www.theblaze.com/stories/2015/01/08/the-reason-the-islamic-faith-bans-images-of-the-prophet-muhammad/, accessed February 14, 2015.
[29] http://www.uscirf.gov/sites/default/files/resources/stories/PDFs/PolicyFocus_USCIRF_final.pdf page 2, accessed February 15, 2015.

remained the same, and Islam was the only religion that had specific attention drawn to it.[30]

After 9/11, the OIC exploited the alleged "backlash" against Muslims and used this as leverage to push for passage of its resolutions. The post 9/11 resolutions took numerous assumptions and asserted them as fact. There were no hearings, debates or investigations to substantiate the claims. Nevertheless, the resolutions assert that Islam is wrongly associated with human rights violations; Islam is wrongly associated with terrorism; and there has been an "intensified campaign" of discrimination, defamation, profiling, and religious hatred waged against Islam and Muslims in the wake of 9/11.[31]

The resolutions further request States to "take action, including through political institutions and organizations, to prohibit the dissemination of racist and xenophobic ideas and material aimed at any religion or its followers that constitute incitement to racial and religious hatred, hostility or violence". They also assert that "respect for religions" and "protection from contempt" is necessary to exercise freedom of thought, conscience and religion.[32] In the OIC's warped view, prohibiting the dissemination of specific ideas, and effectuating State action against it, is compatible with "freedom of opinion and expression."[33]

The resolutions also urge States to "provide adequate protection for acts of hatred... resulting from the defamation of any religion..." and to produce both legal and extra-legal strategies to "combat religious hatred..."[34]

Additionally, while the OIC professes to promote the concept of "combating defamation of religions", it is clear that in its interpretation and implementation, the OIC countries are concerned only with defamation of Islam and Muslims, and not defamation of other religions. Indeed, many of the OIC countries are rife with antisemitism[35], propagated by the governments which foster antisemitic rhetoric in the media. Additionally, anti-infidel stereotypes and discrimination against other

---

[30] http://digitalcommons.law.uga.edu/cgi/viewcontent.cgi?article=1309&context=gjicl pages 351 – 352, accessed December 24, 2014.
[31] See, e.g., http://ap.ohchr.org/documents/E/HRC/resolutions/A_HRC_RES_10_22.pdf, accessed February 15, 2015.
[32] Id. As indicated earlier, the "Combating Defamation of Religions" Resolutions varied slightly in their wording from year to year. The language cited is taken from a combination of the resolutions from 2008-2010, all of which contained the general concepts cited herein.
[33] http://www.volokh.com/posts/1207157234.shtml, accessed December 11, 2014.
[34] http://ap.ohchr.org/documents/E/HRC/resolutions/A_HRC_RES_10_22.pdf, accessed February 15, 2015.
[35] See http://www.jewishvirtuallibrary.org/jsource/myths3/MFtreatment.html, accessed March 9, 2015.

minority religions are weaved throughout societal institutions and the OIC countries are doing nothing to correct this. [36]

To the contrary, many Muslim majority countries that belong to the OIC implement some form of shariah, which affords unequal treatment to Muslims and non-Muslims, with non-Muslims being treated as second class citizens or worse.[37] In Saudi Arabia, for example, one cannot even become a citizen unless Muslim.[38] In Iran, Baha'is are ineligible for government jobs,[39] and in many Muslim countries it is illegal for Christians and Jews to pray in public, to proselytize, or to build and repair churches and synagogues. In Pakistan, it is against the law for Ahmadiyya Muslims to practice their religion, as their version of Islam is considered heretical. If caught, it is a crime punishable by imprisonment.[40]

Though the OIC attempts to clamp down on any freedom of expression that portrays Islam or Muslims negatively, many of its own Member States blatantly discriminate against, punish and violate the human rights of non-Muslims simply based on their faith, while giving preferential treatment to Muslims. And yet, the OIC is pushing for the prohibition of defamation of religions to be considered a "human right" under international law. [41]

Additionally, because of their international nature, the defamation of religions resolutions attempt to usurp national sovereignty on the issue of free speech. America has the First Amendment and other countries have their own rules regarding free expression, but the OIC seeks to replace these laws with what is, in effect, an international blasphemy law.

---

[36] See http://www.newsweek.com/ayaan-hirsi-alithe-global-war-christians-muslim-world-65817, accessed February 15, 2015. Note that the persecution against non-Muslims in OIC countries is not limited to violence by terrorist organizations, but is built upon a system of dhimmitude or second class citizenry imposed by the governments and applied to "people of the book", meaning Jews and Christians. The fate is even worse for those who are not Jews or Christians. This persecution is a function of the Islamist supremacist ideology embraced by the OIC. See, e.g., http://www.discoverthenetworks.org/viewSubCategory.asp?id=41, accessed February 15, 2015 for a general overview of the roots of Islamic Jew-hatred.
[37] Id.
[38] http://www.state.gov/j/drl/rls/irf/2005/51609.htm, accessed December 24, 2014.
[39] http://www.washingtonpost.com/opinions/the-oppression-of-bahais-continues-in-iran/2013/11/12/4b5dcf34-4b0f-11e3-be6b-d3d28122e6d4_story.html, accessed December 10, 2014.
[40] http://www.pakistani.org/pakistan/legislation/1860/actXLVof1860.html section 298, accessed December 24, 2014.
[41] http://islam.ku.dk/lectures/Mayer24112010.pdf pages 2-3, accessed March 3, 2015.

LEGAL STATUS OF UNITED NATIONS RESOLUTIONS

Though UN resolutions do not constitute binding law, signatories to UN resolutions demonstrate political support for the ideas contained in the resolutions. The more often a resolution is passed, the more weight is given to the ideas within the resolution. Repeated passage risks that, at some point, the resolution could be deemed "customary international law",[42] at which point countries that are not signatories to the resolution could be pressured to adhere to it.

---

[42] See http://www.law.cornell.edu/wex/customary_international_law, accessed February 15, 2015.

TIME LINE

The OIC first introduced the Combating Defamation of Religions Resolution to UN Commission on Human Rights in 1999. It introduced a similar resolution to the General Assembly in 2005. The Commission on Human Rights folded in 2005 because the world realized it was a sham. It resurrected under the new name, The Human Rights Council (HRC), in 2006. The Defamation of Religions resolution passed every single year in each of these bodies from the time of its initial introduction through 2010. [43]

As support started to dwindle for the concept of combating defamation of religions, the OIC launched an aggressive Islamophobia campaign to ensure that the resolutions would continue to pass.

The OIC held two major summits on Islamophobia. The first was held in Mecca, Saudi Arabia in 2006. There, the OIC established the existence of "Islamophobia" and announced a zero tolerance for it. The OIC countries asserted that they would defend themselves against all free expression that constitutes Islamophobia, including "hostile glances".[44] They intended to target cartoonists, producers, reporters and governments. They also unveiled their "Ten Year Programme of Action", which included "combating Islamophobia" as a primary goal.[45] This would be achieved largely by persuading the international community to ensure it would "respect all religions and combat their defamation."

At the 2008 Summit, the OIC unveiled the 1st Annual OIC Observatory Report on Islamophobia.[46] This consisted of fifty-eight pages of real, claimed or imagined incidents of Islamophobia. This report is now produced annually. The OIC publishes a Monthly Bulletin on Islamophobia as well.[47]

Many of the so-called "Islamophobic" incidents cited, consist not of bad behavior by non-Muslims toward Muslims, but media reports of the bad acts Muslims have committed toward non-Muslims. In these instances, the mere

---

[43] See http://www.frontpagemag.com/2013/deborah-weiss/u-s-praises-sharia-censorship/, accessed February 15, 2015.
[44] http://iheu.org/discussion-religious-questions-now-banned-un-human-rights-council, accessed December 24, 2014.
[45] http://www.oic-oci.org/oicv2/page/?p_id=228&p_ref=73&lan=en, section VII, accessed December 24, 2014.
[46] http://archive.frontpagemag.com/readArticle.aspx?ARTID=32977, accessed December 25, 2014.
[47] http://www.oic-oci.org/oicv2/page/?p_id=182&p_ref=61&lan=en, accessed December 25, 2014.

reporting of negative behavior on the part of Muslims constitutes "Islamophobia." This definition is dissonant with the Western concept of bigotry. Therefore, it must be understood that the OIC's definition of Islamophobia includes anything that portrays Islam or Muslims in a negative light, including undisputed, accurate factual reports.

Unfortunately, the media often adopts the statistics from Islamophobia tracking organizations without checking into the nature of the claims.[48] The numbers alone can be quite alarming and give a false impression of wide-spread anti-Muslim prejudice.

---

[48] See http://www.wnd.com/2007/12/44961/, accessed February 16, 2015.

THE OIC'S EXAMPLES OF "ISLAMOPHOBIA"

To provide a feel for the nature of the claims that constitute "Islamophobia" in the eyes of the OIC, following are some examples taken from one of the early OIC Islamophobia Monthly Bulletins.

In 2008, Qatar opened its first Christian Church. Muslims protested and Arabic language articles reported the protests. One English language newspaper published a translation of an Arabic article and stated on the header that Muslims protested the opening of the first church. The translated publication was deemed "Islamophobic". [49]

Also cited is Wikipedia's refusal to remove depictions of the Muslims' Prophet Muhammad from its English-language website. The European Union's request that Iran drop the death penalty for the crime of apostasy was also deemed "Islamophobic".

Ever confusing cause with effect, the OIC asserts that Islamophobia is one of the greatest causes of the threat to world peace and global security,[50] rather than concluding that perhaps Islamophobia is the consequence of actions taken by a violent and stealth Islamist movement around the world. 2008 was the first time that the defamation of religions resolution was in danger of not getting passed. However, as a result of the OIC'S Islamophobia victimhood campaign, the resolution passed again, although this time with declining support. [51]

---

[49] http://www.oic-oci.org/english/article/islamophobia-feb08.pdf, accessed November 2008.
[50] http://www.thaindian.com/newsportal/uncategorized/islamophobia-a-threat-to-global-peace-oic-chief-lead_100108474.html, accessed February 16, 2015.
[51] http://www.harvard-jlpp.com/wp-content/uploads/2013/10/LeoFinal.pdf page 770, accessed December 29, 2014.

THE UN HUMAN RIGHTS COUNCIL PASSES A RULE

Subsequently, the HRC implemented a rule which stated that nobody can come before the Human Rights Council and "judge or evaluate" any religion. [52]

The International Humanist Ethical Union (IHEU), raised for consideration, violence against women in Muslim countries. It specifically cited the practices of female genital mutilation, honor killings, stoning for adultery, and forced marriages of little girls.[53]

The IHEU was told that these practices are permissible under shariah, and that therefore the HRC cannot address them because to do so would be to judge or evaluate a religion. It's interesting to note, that the IHEU never mentioned Islam or shariah. Nevertheless, the Egyptian representative declared, "Islam will not be crucified at this Council."[54]

As a result, it appears that human rights violations permitted under shariah, can no longer be discussed in the Human Rights Council, the body purportedly designed to address human rights.

---

[52] http://iheu.org/discussion-religious-questions-now-banned-un-human-rights-council, accessed December 24, 2014.
[53] http://iheu.org/discussion-religious-questions-now-banned-un-human-rights-council/, accessed February 16, 2015.
[54] http://www.jihadwatch.org/2010/04/un-sharia-gate-shipwreck-landmark-revelation-why-fgm-and-violence-against-women-is-taboo, accessed December 29, 2014.

STATE DEPARTMENT REQUEST

Over time, the West caught wind that perhaps the concept of defamation should not be applied to religion. And, the US government began to realize that the defamation of religions resolutions have a potentially catastrophic impact for freedom of speech.

Therefore, in 2011, the State Department requested the OIC to draft an alternative resolution that would preserve freedom of expression[55] and still address the OIC's concerns about alleged Islamophobia.

The result was "Resolution 16/18 to Combat Intolerance Based on Religion or Belief".[56] It was introduced and passed in the Human Rights Council in March 2011. It was the first time in twelve years that the OIC did not introduce the defamation of religions resolution. [57]

The US State Department and numerous NGOs praised the new resolution, believing that the OIC had abandoned its mission to protect Islam from so-called "defamation,"[58] and instead had replaced it with the goal of protecting persecuted religious minorities from discrimination and violence. They assumed the new resolution indicated a paradigm shift, moving away from providing legal protections to an idea or religion and toward providing legal protections for people. However, the title of the new resolution concealed the OIC's true agenda.

---

[55] http://en.islamtoday.net/artshow-235-3990.htm, accessed February 16, 2015.
[56] UN HRC Resolution 16/18: http://www.refworld.org/pdfid/4db960f92.pdf, accessed December 29, 2014.
[57] http://blogs.reuters.com/faithworld/2011/03/24/islamic-bloc-drops-12-year-u-n-drive-to-ban-defamation-of-religion/, accessed December 29, 2014.
[58] http://cnsnews.com/news/article/obama-administration-welcoming-islamic-group-washington-discussion-tolerance, accessed December 29, 2014.

RESOLUTION 16/18: TO COMBAT INTOLERANCE BASED ON RELIGION OR BELIEF

The full title of Resolution 16/18 is "combating intolerance, negative stereotyping and stigmatization of, and discrimination, incitement to violence, and violence against persons based on religion or belief."[59]

Significantly, its language drops the phrase "defamation of religions" and instead focuses on intolerance, negative stereotyping, stereotyping, discrimination, and incitement to violence based on religion or belief.

However, as with any legal document, the language is open to interpretation and in this case, is still problematic.

First, it discourages "religious profiling" for purposes of law enforcement.[60] The resolution defines religious profiling as "the invidious use of religion as a criterion" to conduct interrogations, questioning, searches and investigations. Note that this resolution is not prohibiting the use of religion as the SOLE criterion, but as one factor on a list of other elements to consider. So, if law enforcement suspects there is a plot to commit an Islamic terrorist attack, it would be precluded from taking into account the religion of "persons of interest" in making this determination.

Second, the resolution condemns "the advocacy of religious hatred" that constitutes "incitement to discrimination, hostility or violence". It urges States to take "effective measures" against it when directed towards individuals, and to speak out against it when expressed more generally.[61] These statements are rife with problems. The request for States to take "effective action" against "the advocacy of religious hatred that amounts to incitement to hostility" implies that the manifestation of hatred and hostility should be outlawed. However, hatred and hostility are emotions and cannot be eliminated by government action. Legal systems cannot stamp out emotions and even if they could, outlawing them or criminalizing them is hardly desirable.

Additionally, it has become apparent over time that the OIC's definition of "advocacy of religious hatred" includes criticism of Islam. It is not limited to the advocacy of hatred against individuals. In other words, the OIC imbues the "advocacy of religious hatred" phrase with the same meaning that it gave to "combating

---

[59] UN HRC Resolution 16/18: http://www.refworld.org/pdfid/4db960f92.pdf, accessed December 29, 2014.
[60] Id.
[61] See id.

defamation of religions".[62] It protects the ideology of Islam and prohibits any criticism of it.

Third, the resolution expresses deep concern with the "programs and agendas pursued by extremist groups aimed at perpetuating" these stereotypes. It is evident that the OIC's reference to "extremist groups" does not pertain to terrorist organizations, but so-called "right-wing extremists" including "right wing parties and politicians."[63] The OIC has expressly cited the Tea Party in the U.S.[64] as well as the Freedom Party in the Netherlands, and its leader, MP Geert Wilders, as examples.[65] Other groups that would meet the OIC's criteria for "extremist groups" include the Center for Security Policy, The David Horowitz Freedom Center, and Act for America.

Finally, the most controversial clause in this resolution is its call to "criminalize incitement to imminent violence based on religion or belief".[66] It is clear that the reason the United States agreed to this clause is in part, because it is already illegal in America to incite imminent violence.[67] American and other Western representatives at the UN erroneously believed that signing onto this resolution would preclude the criminalization of ostensibly offensive speech.[68]

At issue is the definition of incitement. Not surprisingly, the OIC's interpretation is again at odds with that applied in the American legal system.

The US uses a "content based test" to determine "incitement". For example, if Sam told his friends to gather together and kill their colleague Joe, and they acted on this, then those who killed Joe would be responsible for murder and Sam would be responsible for incitement to violence because the content of his language encouraged or incited the murder.[69]

---

[62] http://www.nationalreview.com/articles/342072/questionable-victory-free-speech-jacob-mchangama, accessed December 30, 2014.
[63] See http://www.turkishweekly.net/news/122029/norway-attacks-reinforce-need-for-united-stand-against-intolerance.html, accessed December 30, 2014.
[64] http://www.euro-islam.info/wp-content/uploads/pdfs/islamphobia_rep_May_2010_to_April_2011_en.pdf page 16, accessed December 30, 2014.
[65] See Wilders, Geert, "Marked for Death: Islam's War Against the West and Me": https://books.google.com/books?id=Lu25oFwQBeYC&pg=PA207&lpg=PA207&dq=Ihsanoglu+Geert+Wilders&source=bl&ots=hhBuNoRG3o&sig=PJz89Xk2E9ztNgZusdUmSpaNUoA&hl=en&sa=X&ei=PFqjVJiJKoWuggSAm4GgCQ&ved=0CDkQ6AEwBA#v=onepage&q=Ihsanoglu%20Geert%20Wilders&f=false page 207, accessed December 30, 2014.
[66] UN HRC Resolution 16/18: http://www.refworld.org/pdfid/4db960f92.pdf accessed March 3, 2015.
[67] Brandenburg vs Ohio, 395 U.S. 444 (1969).
[68] See https://freedomhouse.org/blog/trouble-blasphemy-laws#.VKNyS6I5B2Y, accessed December 30, 2014.
[69] See Brandenburg vs Ohio, 395 U.S. 444 (1969).

However, the OIC applies a "consequence based test"[70] to the definition of incitement and the example they most frequently cite is that of the Danish cartoons.

In 2005, the Danish newspaper, "Jyllands-Posten", published twelve cartoon illustrations of the Muslim Prophet Muhammad. They were accompanied by an article which debated freedom of speech versus self-censorship. Subsequently, riots ensued all across the Middle East. Danish Embassies were destroyed, and approximately two hundred people were killed.[71] The OIC insists that the riots were the "consequence" of the cartoons.

There are numerous problems with the consequence test.

First, it is a retroactive test. Perfectly legal comments, videos, and cartoons, only become illegal when someone subsequently chooses to act violently in response to them.

Second, the consequence test shifts responsibility from the person who behaves violently to the person who makes a comment, video or cartoon that might be deemed offensive. Note that this shift runs counter to the Judeo-Christian values of personal responsibility, whereby each individual is responsible for his own actions and reactions. In contrast to Islamist violence, Christians have responded to mockery and denigration of sacred Christian symbols primarily through peaceful means. Sometimes the Christian response has included letters to the editor, letters to public officials requesting a denial of public funding for religiously denigrating "art", or the peaceful countering of the offensive viewpoints expressed.[72]

Finally, the application of a consequence-based test enforces the combating defamation of religions concept, the very concept that this resolution purportedly was designed to defeat.

---

[70] http://www.americanthinker.com/articles/2012/12/fatal_attraction_us_flirts_with_international_speech_codes.html, accessed December 30, 2014.
[71] http://www.frontpagemag.com/2014/deborah-weiss/the-tyranny-of-silence/, accessed December 30, 2014.
[72] See http://www.ncregister.com/daily-news/how-to-respond-to-the-last-acceptable-prejudice/, accessed December 31, 2014.

THE OIC'S USE OF PRE-EXISTING LEGAL INSTRUMENTS

A favored OIC tactic is to extract language from pre-existing international legal instruments and insert it into proposed UN resolutions. This makes it more difficult for UN Member States to oppose the resolutions. For example, the International Covenant on Civil and Political Rights (ICCPR) Article 20 (2) states:

> Any advocacy of national, racial or religious hatred that constitutes incitement to discrimination, hostility or violence shall be prohibited by law. [73]

It is evident that the OIC extracted the italicized language from ICCPR Article 20 (2) and inserted it into Resolution 16/18.[74] However, speech restrictions delineated in the ICCPR were intended to apply evenly to all religions. Additionally, a proper understanding of Article 20 provides that it only pertains to hatred directed toward people, not toward religions.[75] Needless to say, the OIC takes this language and exploits it by injecting into it a totally different meaning to suit its own purposes.[76] The OIC applies this language only to Muslims or "Islamophobia" which includes "insults" to the ideology of Islam in addition to people. This completely contravenes the principles of equality and anti-discrimination which were part and parcel of the broader goals of the ICCPR. [77]

Additionally, it is important to note that the Article 20 speech restrictions were opposed by most Western countries. Many made reservations or declarations, in effect exempting themselves form this clause[78] in order to preserve their free speech

---

[73] ICCPR, Article 20(2), http://www.ohchr.org/en/professionalinterest/pages/ccpr.aspx, accessed December 29, 2014.

[74] See UN HRC Resolution 16/18: http://www.refworld.org/pdfid/4db960f92.pdf accessed December 29, 2014.

[75] http://www.uscirf.gov/sites/default/files/resources/stories/PDFs/PolicyFocus_USCIRF_final.pdf page3, accessed January 5, 2015.

[76] The OIC claims that ICCPR Article 20(2) can be used to criminalize the "denigration of religions" as opposed to protecting people.
http://www.saudigazette.com.sa/index.cfm?method=home.regcon&contentid=20130218153611 accessed January 6, 2015.

[77] See ICCPR, Articles 2(1), Article 3, Articles 25 and 25 and to a lesser extent Article 14(1) and Article 14(3): http://www.ohchr.org/en/professionalinterest/pages/ccpr.aspx, accessed February 16, 2015. See also
http://www.uscirf.gov/sites/default/files/resources/stories/PDFs/PolicyFocus_USCIRF_final.pdf page 3, accessed February 16, 2015.

[78] See Leonard Leo, "International Religious Freedom 2010 Annual Report to Congress, page 338 footnote 27:
https://books.google.com/books?id=eYSA2uew3CUC&pg=PA338&lpg=PA338&dq=ICCPR+article+20%282%29+Countries+with+reservations&source=bl&ots=vRCnuQBFdf&sig=QM013_T9EHvXA5fDGq0Rln88qGM&hl=en&sa=X&ei=timrVMehC4qmNq6hhLAG&ved=0CD8

rights as well as their sovereignty on the matter. When the U.S. signed onto the ICCPR, it signed a reservation to this clause.[79] America duly noted that its interpretation would not authorize or require any additional legislation or action by the government and that the First Amendment of the U.S. Constitution would remain the law for American citizens. Therefore, it was unwarranted for the U.S. or other free countries to sign onto this language in Resolution 16/18. Although Resolution 16/18 does not "prohibit by law" the expressions referenced, it lays the groundwork for future legal instruments to gradually tighten the penalties for language that Resolution 16/18 thus far only "condemns".

Second, ICCPR Article 19 (2) states:

> Everyone shall have the right to freedom of expression: this right shall include freedom to seek, receive, and impart information and ideas of all kinds...[80]

Again, Resolution 16/18 mirrors this language, by reaffirming:

> "the positive role that the exercise of the right to freedom of opinion and expression and the full respect for the freedom to seek, receive and impart information can play in strengthening democracy and combating religious intolerance".

The OIC takes the ICCPR language permitting the free flow of information and quickly turns it upside down, implying that "information" should be used to "combat religious intolerance".[81]

It is true that under the ICCPR freedom of expression is guaranteed, but not unlimited. It can be restricted within the parameters defined in Article 19 (3), which reads:

> The exercise of the rights provided for in paragraph 2 of this article carries with it special duties and responsibilities. It may therefore be subject to certain restrictions, but these shall only be such as provided by law and are necessary:
>
> > (a) For respect of the rights or reputations of others;
> >
> > (b) For the protection of national security or of public order (ordre public), or of public health or morals.[82]

Q6AEwBQ#v=onepage&q=ICCPR%20article%2020(2)%20Countries%20with%20reservations&f=false, accessed January 5, 2015.
[79] See http://www.internationaljusticeproject.org/juvICCPR.cfm, accessed January 5, 2015.
[80] ICCPR Article 19(2) http://www.ohchr.org/en/professionalinterest/pages/ccpr.aspx accessed December 29, 2014.
[81] UN HRC Resolution 16/18, http://www.refworld.org/pdfid/4db960f92.pdf, accessed December 29, 2014.
[82] ICCPR Article 19(3), http://www.ohchr.org/en/professionalinterest/pages/ccpr.aspx, accessed December 29, 2014.

However, the traditional understanding of Article 19 requires a broad construction of the right to free expression and a narrow construction of its limitations.[83] Conversely, Resolution 16/18 reveals the OIC's erroneously narrow interpretation of "free expression" and contempt for free speech. At the same time, it gives the restrictions on free speech an overly broad construction. Resolution 16/18 acknowledges the right to free expression. But hypocritically, it then proceeds to condemn, deplore, or "note with deep concern" speech designated offensive and aspires to implement action to effectuate its suppression.[84]

In numerous other speeches and documents outside the scope of Resolution 16/18, the OIC repeatedly mimics the restrictive language of ICCPR Article 19, injecting it with a meaning it was never intended to have.[85]

Further, the OIC seeks to impose this unfounded interpretation on general human rights law and international law. The truth is that there is no basis in human rights law for the implementation of blasphemy statutes or their equivalent. The restriction of freedom of speech considered "blasphemous" is anti-Constitutional[86] and antithetical to international standards of genuine human rights.[87]

---

[83] http://eclj.org/pdf/eclj_draftgeneralcommentno34-article19_20110201.pdf pages 4-5, accessed February 28, 2015.
[84] UN HRC Resolution 16/18, http://www.refworld.org/pdfid/4db960f92.pdf, accessed December 29, 2014.
[85] See, e.g., http://www.turkishweekly.net/news/122029/norway-attacks-reinforce-need-for-united-stand-against-intolerance.html accessed January 6, 2015. Additionally, many of the OIC Annual Islamophobia Reports and OIC speeches and articles are replete with commentary indicating that free speech comes with "duties and responsibilities" which, in context, clearly means censorship on Islam-related topics.
[86] See Burstyn v. Wilson, 342 U.S. 495 at pages 504-505, (1952).
[87] See http://eclj.org/pdf/eclj_draftgeneralcommentno34-article19_20110201.pdf pages 6-7, accessed March 1, 2015.

THE DEFINITION OF ISLAMOPHOBIA

The word "Islamophobia" only came into the English lexicon in recent decades.[88] Westerners have naively assumed a definition that implies bigotry or prejudice against Muslims. Accordingly, its usage is often equated with sexism, racism and other types of discrimination.[89]

However, according to the OIC, anyone who "defames Islam" is an "Islamophobe". Because the OIC's definition of "defamation" is tantamount to Islamic blasphemy, when the OIC uses the word "Islamophobia" it encompasses much more than the American notion of mere bigotry.[90] It also includes any factual discussion of Islamic terrorism, Islamic persecution of religious minorities, and human rights violations committed in the name of Islam.[91]

In other words, the OIC has deftly managed to conflate notions of bigotry and prejudice with legitimate statements of fact. This has led to a false and exaggerated impression of Islamophobia, as a greatly widespread and pervasive prejudice against Muslims. The OIC has also proffered the unsubstantiated idea that hate speech leads to violence.[92] These false premises are then used as a basis to argue for and legitimize speech restrictions.

Though there is some discrimination against Muslims as there is with other groups, the OIC's application of the word Islamophobia is nothing more than pretext for censorship.[93] It is intended to chill the speech of those accused of it. Still, the "elimination" of Islamophobia remains a matter of utmost priority for the OIC.[94]

---

[88] See http://www.discoverthenetworks.org/viewSubCategory.asp?id=777, accessed December 29, 2014.
[89] See http://www.americanthinker.com/blog/2008/03/vote_mccain_and_youre_a_sexist.html, accessed February 17, 2015.
[90] See www.oic-un.org/document_report/observatory_report_final.doc, accessed January 1, 2015.
[91] See, e.g., http://ap.ohchr.org/documents/E/HRC/resolutions/A_HRC_RES_7_19.pdf, accessed January 1, 2015. (This resolution proposes that the equating of a religion with terrorism should always be rejected, apparently without regard to the truth or falsity of the claim.)
[92] See http://www.todayszaman.com/op-ed_freedom-of-expression-is-not-a-license-to-incite-hatred-and-intolerance-1-by-ekmeleddin-ihsanoglu-_289645.html, accessed January 1, 2014.
[93] See www.oic-un.org/document_report/observatory_report_final.doc pages 1, 3, 5, accessed January 1, 2015.
[94] See http://www.euro-islam.info/wp-content/uploads/pdfs/islamphobia_rep_May_2010_to_April_2011_en.pdf page 1, accessed January 1, 2015.

Further, the OIC is determined to have the international community pick up, prioritize, and enforce this same cause.[95]

The OIC is also pushing to criminalize "Islamophobia" by working to have it defined as "racism". For example, the International Convention on the Elimination of All Forms of Racial Discrimination (ICERD) is an international legally binding document that prohibits discrimination based on race, color, national origin, descent, or ethnicity.[96] However, the OIC insists that this UN Convention should play a role in eliminating "contemporary forms of racism".[97] The OIC defines "contemporary racism" as discrimination based on culture, belief or religion, with an emphasis on religion, especially Islam.[98] This turns the whole concept of racial discrimination prohibitions on its head. The underlying premise of anti-discrimination laws is that people are all equal and should not be treated disparately based on immutable characteristics.[99] However, characteristics which are changeable and demonstrate values, should be subject to scrutiny, evaluation and when warranted, criticism.

Finally, the OIC's definition of "intolerance" includes tolerance of the intolerant views inherent in shariah. Therefore, "combating intolerance" or "Islamophobia" pursuant to Resolution 16/18, includes more than the protection of Muslims, but extends to the protection of Islam itself.

Thus, while Resolution 16/18 has altered the defamation of religions language, the OIC has made it clear that it has not dropped its goal to combat defamation of Islam.[100]

---

[95] Id.
[96] ICCPR, Article I, paragraph 1, http://www.ohchr.org/EN/ProfessionalInterest/Pages/CERD.aspx, accessed January 15, 2015.
[97] See http://www.harvard-jlpp.com/wp-content/uploads/2013/10/LeoFinal.pdf page 775, accessed March 3, 2015.
[98] See, e.g., www.oic-un.org/document_report/observatory_report_final.doc OIC Secretary General Ihsanoglu's Foreward, pages 1-3.
[99] http://www.uscirf.gov/sites/default/files/resources/stories/PDFs/PolicyFocus_USCIRF_final.pdf page 6, accessed January 15, 2015.
[100] http://www.thecommentator.com/article/4345/west_must_stop_appeasing_efforts_to_ban_criticism_of_islam, accessed February 17, 2015.

SECRETARY CLINTON'S ANNOUNCEMENT OF THE ISTANBUL PROCESS

In July 2011, OIC Secretary-General Ekmeleddin Ihsanoglu and US Secretary of State Hillary Clinton co-chaired a high level diplomatic meeting on Islamophobia held in Istanbul, Turkey. The meeting was also attended by Catherine Ashton, Foreign Representative for the European Union, as well as by the Vatican, the Arab League, and numerous foreign ministers and officials from stakeholder countries around the world.[101]

At this meeting, the co-chairs launched an initiative to "move to implementation" Resolution 16/18, in order to make it a reality. Participants at the meeting vowed to go beyond "mere rhetoric" and reaffirmed their commitment to conduct activities and events to implement the resolution.[102] Secretary Clinton specifically announced that the US State Department would hold a conference to start the process[103] despite the fact that nothing in the resolution mandates this and it is contrary to the norm of leaving UN Resolutions in the realm of the hypothetical. This implementation process became known as the "Istanbul Process".[104]

Indeed, the State Department did hold the first international Istanbul conference in December, 2011.[105] It thereby gave credence to the OIC's goals and indicated to the Free World that partnership with the OIC is not only acceptable, but perhaps even desirable.

The European Union held the second Istanbul Conference in December of 2012.[106] Subsequently, the third conference in the Istanbul series was held in Geneva, in June of 2013[107] and the fourth conference was held in Doha, Qatar in March of 2014.[108]

Accordingly, the OIC Secretary General touted the Istanbul Process as the "a poster child for OIC-US-EU cooperation."[109]

---

[101] http://geneva.usmission.gov/2011/07/18/joint-statement-on-combating-intolerance-discrimination-and-violence/, accessed March 3, 2015.
[102] Id.
[103] http://www.foxnews.com/politics/2011/11/11/free-speech-concerns-ahead-meeting-with-muslim-nations-on-religious-tolerance/#ixzz1dQRSf1QN, accessed March 3, 2015.
[104] http://www.thecommentator.com/article/4345/west_must_stop_appeasing_efforts_to_ban_criticism_of_islam, accessed February 17, 2015.
[105] http://cnsnews.com/news/article/state-dept-aims-denounce-offensive-speech-while-upholding-free-expression, accessed March 3, 2015.
[106] See http://www.thewashingtonreview.org/articles/will-istanbul-process-relieve-the-tension-between-the-muslim-world-and-the-west.html, accessed March 3, 2015.
[107] Id.
[108] http://www.academia.edu/10450135/Doha_Meeting_Report_for_Advancing_Religious_Freedom_2014, accessed March 9, 2015.
[109] Id.

THE US STATE DEPARTMENT ISTANBUL CONFERENCE

The US State Department held the first Istanbul conference in December, 2011. It took place over a three day period and consisted primarily of closed-door sessions. Approximately thirty countries and international organizations participated, including the US, the EU, and the OIC.[110]

After passage of Resolution 16/18, Secretary Clinton asserted that the resolution shows "we have begun to overcome the false divide that pits religious sensitivities against freedom of expression."[111]

Nevertheless, the OIC made it clear that its goals for the conference were to push for speech restrictive measures on Islam-related topics and to focus on eliminating "Islamohobia" in the West.[112]

Instead of emphasizing the protection of free expression, the conference zeroed in on the prevention of discrimination and "intolerance" against religious minorities. Specifically, the focus was on the alleged intolerance of Muslims in the West,[113] despite the fact that they are free and equal in the eyes of the law. The problem of truly persecuted Jews (if there are any left) and Christians in Saudi Arabia, Ahmadiyya Muslims in Pakistan, Coptic Christians in Egypt, and Baha'is in Iran, all went unaddressed. [114]

Secretary Clinton asserted that the US would not push for the enactment of speech-restrictive laws (at least for the time being), and she extolled the virtues of free speech.[115] But she also proclaimed that the US advocates for other measures to achieve the same results. Those other measures included interfaith dialogue and the use of "good old fashioned techniques of peer pressure and shaming."[116] In other words, Secretary Clinton supports government efforts to suppress free speech, so long as the means to achieve it is social pressure and political correctness, rather than legislation.

---

[110] See http://cnsnews.com/news/article/obama-administration-welcoming-islamic-group-washington-discussion-tolerance, accessed March 3, 2015.
[111] http://english.alarabiya.net/articles/2011/07/16/157826.html, accessed March 3, 2015.
[112] http://www.nationalreview.com/article/276021/administration-takes-islamophobia-nina-shea, accessed March 9, 2015.
[113] See http://www.investigativeproject.org/3355/state-department-panders-to-islamists-on-free#, accessed March 3, 2015.
[114] See, e.g., http://m.nationalreview.com/corner/285654/dc-islamophobia-conference-was-bad-idea-nina-shea, accessed February 17, 2015.
[115] http://www.state.gov/secretary/20092013clinton/rm/2011/12/178866.htm, accessed January 29, 2015.
[116] Id.

However, it is not the proper role of the State Department to stifle the speech of Americans with whom it disagrees, using social means or otherwise. To the contrary, it is beyond the purview of all US government entities to suppress free expression, however unpopular.

The United States Constitution's First Amendment states: [117]

> Congress shall make no law respecting an establishment of religion, or prohibiting the free exercise thereof; or abridging the freedom of speech, or of the press; or the right of the people peaceably to assemble, and to petition the Government for a redress of grievances.

The First Amendment was designed to encourage robust political debate and flesh out minority viewpoints.[118] It was enacted, in part, to protect offensive speech. If it protected only polite speech or speech with which all were in agreement, the First Amendment would not be necessary.

While government policies designed to inhibit free expression might not violate the letter of law, they clearly violate the spirit of the law.

Secretary Clinton explained that she wants to "bridge the divide"[119] that separates different faiths and cultures. The problem is the bridge of tolerance flows in only one direction: toward the Islamization of the West, and the shrinking of free expression.

---

[117] http://www.history.org/history/teaching/enewsletter/volume8/nov09/images/plaintext_billofrights.pdf, accessed January 15, 2015.
[118] See http://www.bc.edu/bc_org/avp/cas/comm/free_speech/nytvsullivan.html, accessed February 26, 2015.
[119] http://www.state.gov/secretary/20092013clinton/rm/2011/07/168636.htm, accessed March 3, 2015.

THE PROCESS OF LOSING FREEDOM OF SPEECH

Many people believe that restrictions on freedom of speech will never be implemented in America because we have the First Amendment. Certainly, the loss of free speech will not occur over night. However, even in America, the permanency of freedom is not inevitable and ought not be taken for granted. All it would require is for Congress to pass a hate speech law (and the idea has been tossed around), and for five Supreme Court Justices to hold that the First Amendment does not apply to hate speech, the same way it does not apply to defamation of individuals or other First Amendment exceptions. In that case, "hate speech" would become outlawed, no matter how erroneous the judicial ruling might be. What "hate speech" would encompass would remain to be seen, but negative opinions and unpleasant truths would undoubtedly be targeted.

Freedom is not the normal state of the world. It is the exception. The process of losing freedom does not have to occur in a violent coup. It can be lost slowly, due the gradual erosion of values, societal complacency and the incremental chipping away at laws that protect freedom, as well as the passage of laws that destroy it.[120]

Threats to freedom must be identified early on, and be named by name in order to address them before it's too late.

The gradual and incremental loss of freedom occurs in stages. The first stage is self-censorship. It begins with people societal pressure urging people to use "sensitive speech", "politically correct speech" or "responsible speech". [121]

Next, governments and institutions lay out speech restrictive guidelines and policies. These circumstances up the ante because authoritative institutions issue directives, even if they don't constitute legal prohibitions. Examples in this category include colleges and federal agencies that instruct students and employees to refrain from certain types of language.[122]

The next step is to create civil laws or regulations that prohibit free expression. This can take the form of legislation, such as "hate speech" laws or such laws can be applied by government agencies that adopt their own regulations, whether

---

[120] See https://faithandfreedomfootnotes.wordpress.com/2012/07/20/freedom-is-lost-gradually/, accessed February 26, 2015.
[121] See, e.g., http://www.chicagotribune.com/news/opinion/commentary/ct-cartoonists-rights-free-speech-paris-perspec-0109-20150108-story.html, accessed February 26, 2015.
[122] See, e.g., http://archive.frontpagemag.com/readArticle.aspx?ARTID=31840, accessed February 26, 2015.

or not those regulations comport with the nation's constitution. If the laws are antithetical to the Constitution or official legislation, the agency administering the regulations can operate as a parallel court system. An example of this is the Canadian Human Rights Commissions, which hold hearings independently from the nation's courts. Until very recently, a finding of liability on so-called hate speech was penalized with a fine.[123]

The last step in the process is the criminalization of speech. In this instance, prohibited speech is deemed an offense against the State and can be prosecuted. Those who are charged with criminal speech in the West, face the possibility of fines or imprisonment.[124] In totalitarian countries as well as Islamic theocracies, the punishments are even harsher, resulting in jail, flogging, or even execution.[125]

---

[123] See, e.g., http://archive.frontpagemag.com/readArticle.aspx?ARTID=32062, accessed February 26, 2015.
[124] See, e.g., http://www.legal-project.org/issues/geert-wilders, accessed February 26, 2015.
[125] See, e.g., http://www.rationalistinternational.net/Shaikh/blasphemy_laws_in_pakistan.htm, accessed February 26, 2015.

ADDITIONAL ANALYSIS

Free speech constitutes a human right. It is a foundational precept for liberty.[126] Only people should be afforded human rights. Ideas, policies and religions should not be afforded legal protection from criticism.

Additionally, the OIC intentionally conflates the concept of "combating defamation of religions" with religious liberty.[127] However, the two are not the same. Religious freedom is a right that belongs to an individual or group of individuals.[128] It is not the right of a religion itself. [129]

The OIC cloaks its ideas in the language of freedom and aspires to have "combating defamation of religions" deemed a human right.[130] In reality, the opposite is true. Where ever ideas are protected from criticism in the form of government imposed censorship, human rights abuses run rampant.[131]

For that reason, it is imperative to place the emphasis on individual rights as opposed to group rights or the rights of ideas and religions. The OIC, conversely, has as its priorities the rights of the Islamic Ummah[132] and of supremacist Islam, often at

---

[126] See http://eclj.org/pdf/eclj_draftgeneralcommentno34-article19_20110201.pdf page 6, accessed March 9, 2015.

[127] See http://web.archive.org/web/20090206220325/http://www.becketfund.org/files/73099.pdf page 6, accessed February 14, 2015. See also discussion by Paul Marshall & Nina Shea, "Silenced: How Apostasy and Blasphemy Codes are Choking Freedom Worldwide", pages 4 and 206, Oxford University Press, 2011. In a myriad of documents, the OIC conflates religious freedom protections for individuals with protection of Islam from "defamation", implying that protecting Islam from "defamation" constitutes a religious freedom.

[128] See UN Declaration of Human Rights, Article 18, http://www.un.org/en/documents/udhr/, accessed March 9, 2015.

[129] See http://www.refworld.org/docid/45c30b640.html paragraph 27, accessed January 2, 2015.

[130] http://www.euro-islam.info/wp-content/uploads/pdfs/islamphobia_rep_May_2010_to_April_2011_en.pdf page 29, accessed February 14, 2015. See also http://gatesofvienna.blogspot.com/2012/11/the-state-department-moves-istanbul.html, accessed February 14, 2015.

[131] See http://www.humanrightsfirst.org/resource/compendium-blasphemy-laws, accessed January 2, 2015.

[132] See http://www.oic-oci.org/oicv2/page/?p_id=53&p_ref=27&lan=en, accessed February 14, 2015.

the expense of the individual.[133] Its framework is totally at odds with Western notions of individual rights and individual liberty.

The OIC claims it wants "respect", but what it really demands is "compliance" from non-Muslim countries.[134] Make no mistake about it: the OIC's campaign to combat defamation of religions is aimed at the West to suppress speech critical only of Islam.[135] Its Member States have shown no concern for the "defamation" of Christianity, Judaism, or other minority religions in the OIC countries.

To the contrary, the Defamation of Religions Resolutions and Resolution 16/18, are used to justify domestic blasphemy laws and the persecution of religious minorities in the OIC countries.[136]

Though the OIC changed its rhetoric with the introduction of Resolution 16/18, its liberty-crushing objectives remain unchanged. [137] Using softer and more "feel-good" words, the OIC has embarked on a mission to silence critics of anything about Islam, under the guise of "tolerance" and "plurality". [138]

Clearly, the OIC's language change is nothing more than tactical.[139] Even a superficial glance at the laws in the OIC countries will prove that the OIC countries are anything but tolerant. Indeed, the OIC as well as the UN Human Rights Council, consist of some of the most egregious human rights violators in the world.[140]

The OIC resolutions to restrict freedom of speech have negative repercussions for national security, terrorism prevention efforts, religious freedom,

---

[133] See http://www.americanthinker.com/articles/2008/12/human_rights_vs_islamic_rights.html, accessed February 14, 2015.

[134] See http://www.washingtontimes.com/news/2009/oct/30/a-demand-for-respect/?page=all, accessed March 9, 2015.

[135] See http://www.gatestoneinstitute.org/3474/blasphemy-laws-europe, accessed January 2, 2015. See also https://thejihadproject.files.wordpress.com/2012/02/001_islamphobia_rep_may_07_08.pdf pages 1-10, accessed January 2, 2015.

[136] http://www.uscirf.gov/sites/default/files/resources/stories/PDFs/PolicyFocus_USCIRF_final.pdf page 1, accessed February 14, 2015.

[137] http://www.thecommentator.com/article/4345/west_must_stop_appeasing_efforts_to_ban_criticism_of_islam, accessed February 15, 2015.

[138] http://jonathanturley.org/2011/12/13/criminalizing-intolerance-obama-administration-moves-forward-on-united-nations-resolution-targeting-anti-religious-speech/, accessed February 26, 2015.

[139] See http://www.thecommentator.com/article/4345/west_must_stop_appeasing_efforts_to_ban_criticism_of_islam, accessed February 26, 2015.

[140] See https://freedomhouse.org/report/freedom-world/freedom-world-2010?page=363&year=2010#.VMwpyaI5B2Y, accessed January 30, 2015.

and human rights. The implementation of these resolutions is shrinking Western liberty rather than expanding freedom in the Middle East and the rest of the world.

There is nothing virtuous about being tolerant of the intolerant. And there is no justification for censoring truth, however unpleasant it might be. Capitulating to Islamist theocracies has consequences. The policy prohibitions against using certain verbiage serve two purposes from the OIC's standpoint. First, the prohibitions mandate non-Muslims to comply with the equivalent of Islamic blasphemy codes in accordance with shariah, inherently demonstrating the subordination of their own freedoms and laws. Second, they serve to prevent the West from being informed about Islamist goals for dominance and provide a veneer of protection for Islamic terrorist groups as well as Islamic human rights violators. If the motivations and goals of these groups cannot be acknowledged or discussed, including the goals of the OIC, then the West cannot effectively produce a strategy to combat them. The language prohibitions are not merely intended to stifle speech, but serve as thought-stopping measures designed to confuse, obscure, and aid in fogging the war to Islamist's advantage.

REAL LIFE CONSEQUENCES OF PUTTING INTO EFFECT THE COMBATING DEFAMATION OF RELIGIONS CONCEPT

The OIC's success in advancing its cause to "combat defamation of Islam" is alarming[141] and has real life consequences which manifest in the significant reduction of freedom.

The following examples demonstrate the manifestations of the how "combating defamation of Islam" is applied in practice. These are not necessarily the direct result of the OIC's UN resolutions or the OIC itself, but merely demonstrate applications of the concept.

1. Virtually every country in the Europe, as well as Australia, now has some form of speech restrictive laws.[142] Some of the countries have hate speech laws, laws prohibiting the denigration of religions, or public order laws. All of these laws serve the same purpose as Islamic blasphemy laws by deterring speech critical of Islam and punishing it when it occurs. [143]

2. Canada has a constitution that affords citizens free speech. Yet until recently, for years there were Human Rights Commissions in almost every province that acted as parallel courts, regularly issuing civil fines for criticizing Islam.[144]

3. Dutch Member of Parliament, Geert Wilders has explained that he is opposed to the ideology of Islam, but does not hate Muslims.[145] Despite this, he was criminally prosecuted for merely expressing his opinion. The language of the Dutch Penal Code, under which he was charged, is similar to that of Resolution 16/18 focusing on incitement of hatred. Eventually, he

---

[141] http://jonathanturley.org/2011/12/13/criminalizing-intolerance-obama-administration-moves-forward-on-united-nations-resolution-targeting-anti-religious-speech/, accessed February 26, 2015.
[142] See, e.g., http://eur-lex.europa.eu/legal-content/EN/ALL/?uri=CELEX:32008F0913, accessed January 31, 2015.
[143] See Paul Marshall and Nina Shea, "Silenced: How Apostasy & Blasphemy Codes are Choking Freedom Worldwide, Oxford University Press, 2011 at page 235.
[144] Civil prosecutions were executed under Section 13 of the Canadian Human Rights Act: http://laws-lois.justice.gc.ca/eng/acts/H-6/section-13-20021231.html, accessed January 31, 2015. This provision was repealed effective June 27, 2013. See http://news.nationalpost.com/2012/06/07/jonathan-kay-good-riddance-to-section-13-of-the-canadian-human-rights-act/, accessed January 31, 2015.
[145] http://www.theguardian.com/world/2008/feb/17/netherlands.islam, accessed January 31, 2015.

was acquitted,[146] but the mere prosecution for expressing opinions in a non-Muslim, supposedly free country has a chilling effect on free speech.[147]

4. In America, US federal agencies charged with fighting the War on Terror, including the FBI, CIA, Department of Homeland Security, the State Department and the National Counterterrorism Center, have all purged their national security training material from any mention of Islamic terrorism or Islamist ideology.[148] Consultants who trained counterterrorism professionals for years have been dropped from government contracts.[149]

5. The National Security Strategy Memo, our country's guiding document for all national security policy, previously asserted that "militant Islamic radicalism is the greatest ideological conflict of the 21st century".[150] This statement has been dropped in the current version of the Memo and all mention of Islamist threats has been purposely omitted.[151]

6. The Department of Homeland Security Advisory Committee (HSAC) advised DHS to instruct its national security professionals to focus on terrorist behavior and "de-link" it from its motivating ideology.[152]

7. Additionally, the Department of Homeland Security, and other federal agencies have issued memos to their national security and counterterrorism professionals discouraging them from using a host of words including Islam, jihad or Islamic terrorism, despite the fact that the agencies admit the accuracy of the terms.[153]

8. In the past, whenever UN documents had a provision that restricted free speech, the US signed a reservation or declaration effectively opting out of

---

[146] Wilders was charged for "insulting to a group of people based on their race, their religion or belief" and for "inciting hatred against or discrimination of" Muslims. http://www.legal-project.org/issues/geert-wilders, accessed January 31, 2015.

[147] At the time of this writing, Wilders is expected to go on trial again, this time at The Hague, for comments he made at a March 19, 1014 rally, calling for a reduction in immigration of Moroccan Muslims. The charges are made pursuant to the same statutory language his prior trial. See http://www.dailymail.co.uk/news/article-2878776/Dutch-populist-Wilders-tried-fewer-Moroccans-vow.html, accessed March 9, 2015.

[148] See, e.g., http://www.frontpagemag.com/2011/robert-spencer/obama-adminstration-bans-the-truth-about-islam-and-jihad/, accessed January 31, 2015.

[149] See http://www.clarionproject.org/analysis/muslim-brotherhood-takes-charge-fbi-counterterrorism-training, accessed January 31, 2015.

[150] https://www.ascfusa.org/news_posts/view/951, accessed February 26, 2015.

[151] Id.

[152] See https://www.dhs.gov/xlibrary/assets/hsac_cve_working_group_recommendations.pdf page 5, accessed March 9, 2015.

[153] http://archive.frontpagemag.com/readArticle.aspx?ARTID=31840, accessed February 26, 2015.

that clause, adhering to the primacy of the First Amendment.[154] Now, the US State Department is spearheading the implementation of speech restrictive measures similar to those the US government previously disavowed.[155] This demonstrates a dramatic change over the years in the government's stance on the importance of free speech.

9. Indeed, in November of 2012, subsequent to the assumed shift away from the "combating defamation of religions" concept, the US sent State Department representative Ann Casper, to participate in an OIC symposium on "combating defamation of Islam" held in Saudi Arabia.[156] There, the OIC failed to extend even the pretense of even-handedness toward other religions.

---

[154] See http://www.internationaljusticeproject.org/juvICCPR.cfm, accessed January 5, 2015.
[155] See http://cnsnews.com/news/article/obama-administration-welcoming-islamic-group-washington-discussion-tolerance, accessed March 3, 2015.
[156] http://www.breitbart.com/national-security/2012/11/19/obama-official-attends-oic-meeting-on-defamation-of-islam/, accessed January 2, 2015.

THE OBAMA ADMINISTRATION'S PURPOSEFUL DENIAL OF ALL THINGS ISLAM

There are numerous instances where the Obama Administration has demonstrated a total unwillingness to acknowledge the existence of Islamic terrorism, even if it's expressly dissociated from "all Muslims" or "all interpretations of Islam". This is to the detriment of America's national security.[157] Often the denial goes beyond ignoring the facts, and consists of active support for the faux innocence of anything Islam-related.

For example, it is well established at this point, that the events which occurred in Benghazi constituted a terrorist attack committed by an Al-Qaeda affiliate,[158] and not a "spontaneous uprising" as the Administration originally claimed. The Administration disingenuously blamed the attacks on an obscure, low-budget video about the life of Muhammad.[159] In addition to the underlying facts that transpired, a question arises about why the Administration chose scapegoating the video as the *means* of the cover up. It is likely that it was intended to serve a dual purpose by appeasing the Muslim world and demonstrating that America, too, is working hard to protect Islam from "defamation."

While testifying at a Congressional hearing, Attorney General Eric Holder stumbled on his words when asked a question about Al-Qaeda's motivating ideology. Congressman Lamar Smith, Ranking Member of the House Judiciary Committee noted that those who committed recent terrorist attacks had ties to Islam and asked if it was possible that they were motived by radical Islam. Holder replied, "There are a variety of reasons why…" The question was repeated: "Could radical Islam have been one of the reasons?" The Attorney General was unwilling to provide a straight forward "yes" even when the question was couched with numerous qualifiers.[160]

To the contrary, there have been numerous times when Administration officials have insisted that "Islam is a religion of peace"[161] and that no version of Islam could ever preach hatred or violence, despite the fact that none of the officials have theological expertise.

---

[157] See https://www.ascfusa.org/news_posts/view/951, accessed February 26, 2015.
[158] http://www.thedailybeast.com/articles/2012/09/26/u-s-officials-knew-libya-attacks-were-work-of-al-qaeda-affiliates.html, accessed January 29, 2015.
[159] http://townhall.com/columnists/katiepavlich/2012/10/25/the_deadly_consequences_of_the_white_house_blaming_a_video_for_benghazi/page/full, accessed January 29, 2015.
[160] https://www.youtube.com/watch?v=HOQt_mP6Pgg, accessed December 9, 2014.
[161] http://dailycaller.com/2014/09/03/kerry-the-real-face-of-islam-is-a-peaceful-religion-video/, accessed January 29, 2015.

Indeed, in his 2009 Cairo speech, which included invited audience members of the Muslim Brotherhood, President Obama declared that is it part of his job as President of the United States to "fight negative stereotypes of Islam wherever they appear".[162] It is important to note that he alluded to the ideology of Islam, rather than to Muslims. Furthermore, no such Presidential duty is even remotely referenced in the United States Constitution.

In 2012, President Obama, again referring to the "Innocence of Muslims" video trailer, stated at the United Nations: "The future must not belong to those that slander the Prophet of Islam."[163] Additionally, the U.S. State Department paid approximately 70,000 dollars for public service announcements in Pakistan to inform the Pakistani public that America denounced the video about Muhammad.[164]

In 2014, when speaking about The Islamic State or "IS", the President asserted that IS has nothing to do with Islam; nor is it a State.[165] He thus tipped off the audience that he is either woefully ignorant of Islamist motivations to establish a Caliphate (which would rule over a global Nation of Islam, but would not recognize "manmade territorial boundaries") or that he is intentionally misleading the American public.

There are numerous other examples as well.

---

[162] http://www.whitehouse.gov/the-press-office/remarks-president-cairo-university-6-04-09, accessed January 27, 2015.
[163] https://www.youtube.com/watch?v=T6uZFSj_ueM, accessed January 27, 2015.
[164] http://worldnews.nbcnews.com/_news/2012/09/20/13992235-us-spends-70000-on-pakistan-ad-denouncing-anti-muslim-film?lite, accessed January 27, 2015.
[165] http://www.washingtonpost.com/blogs/the-fix/wp/2014/09/11/obama-says-the-islamic-state-is-not-islamic-americans-are-inclined-to-disagree/, accessed January 27, 2015.

WHAT AMERICA SHOULD BE DOING

First and foremost, the United States Constitution's enumerated powers issue a clear mandate for the federal government to protect the security of its citizens. It is additionally the proper function of the government to act as the steward of freedom for Americans.[166] Keeping both the supremacy of the United States Constitution and the principles upon which this country was founded as foremost priorities, the US government should refrain from acquiescing to outside influences which would undermine its proper mission.[167] It should especially resist the temptation to capitulate to countries and NGOs that have dissonant values, as demonstrated through the implementation of those values in their own countries.

The US State Department should stop collaborating with the OIC, thereby giving it legitimacy.[168] It should terminate its participation in "combating defamation of Islam" seminars abroad, as well as halt the Istanbul Process here at home. This means putting an end to the whitewashing of Islamic terrorism, re-installing proper training for counterterrorism and law enforcement officials, and retracting word list bans for agencies that should be fighting the Global Jihad Movement.[169] Indeed, the State Department needs a total overhaul of its positions regarding various "interfaith dialogue," "Muslim outreach" and "anti-profiling" policies and programs to realistically line them up with threats facing the United States, rather than promoting political correctness at security's expense.[170]

The United States government should stop relating to the OIC from a defensive stance and develop a strategy of offense instead. America should be standing on principle for freedom of speech and advocating for the equivalent of a worldwide First Amendment. At the United Nations, America should refrain from signing onto

---

[166] See the United States Constitution, Article I, Section 8.
[167] The Obama Administration has been working with Islamist organizations in developing its national security and foreign policy. See, e.g., http://www.washingtontimes.com/blog/watercooler/2012/sep/24/picket-muslim-advocacy-groups-influence-heavily-us/, accessed February 28, 2015.
[168] http://www.frontpagemag.com/2011/deborah-weiss/saudi-arabia-and-the-global-islamic-terrorist-network/, accessed February 28, 2015.
[169] Word list bans were discussed previously in this monograph to demonstrate how the concept of "combating defamation of Islam" is being implemented. See, e.g., http://archive.frontpagemag.com/readArticle.aspx?ARTID=31840, accessed February 28, 2015.
[170] Federal agencies including the FBI, CIA, DHS, DOJ, NCTC and the State Department should also cut all ties with Muslim Brotherhood front groups. For an example of the Obama Administration's Muslim outreach, see http://www.state.gov/r/pa/ei/biog/230768.htm, accessed February 28, 2015.

OIC UN resolutions or at least sign reservations acknowledging the right of US citizens to retain freedom of expression consistent with the United States' Constitution's First Amendment. When OIC resolutions come up for a vote, instead of praising the OIC for upholding a so-called "consensus" on Resolution 16/18, America should join Ireland and other outspoken countries that denounce potential censorship of the press and espouse open debate on all topics.[171] US officials should be holding America up as a shining example of freedom to be emulated by the rest of the world instead of apologizing for phony prejudices and making our country subservient to the ideals of tyrannical regimes.

Additionally, America should denounce the OIC countries that implement blasphemy and apostasy laws.[172] The US should pressure them to replace those laws with the human rights of free expression and freedom of religion, including the freedom to leave a religion, change religions or have no religion.

The State Department and other U.S. agencies should also be condemning additional human rights violations perpetrated by OIC countries including Iran, Saudi Arabia, Sudan, and Pakistan. America must insist that "combating defamation of religions" is not deemed a human right.

America should also withdraw from the UN Human Rights Council, which is nothing more than a sham used by human rights violators to provide each other with cover.[173] The US should advocate for a requirement which disallows countries with egregious human rights records from being seated on the Council.[174]

If the US continues to provide money to OIC countries that implement shariah in whole or in part, then the money should be conditioned on specific human rights requirements rather than a carte blanche gift.

Congress must continue to ensure freedom of expression for its citizens and guard against the passage of any laws that smack of censorship including hate speech laws or laws prohibiting the denigration of religions. The proper way to counter bad ideas is with good ideas, not censorship.

---

[171] Reference speeches by both the US and EU Ambassadors to the UN here: http://webtv.un.org/watch/ahrc221-40-vote-item9-50th-meeting-22nd-regular-session-%20humanightsouncil/2245193180001?utm_source=twitterfeed&utm_medium=twitter, accessed February 28, 2015.
[172] Pakistan, Saudi Arabia, Iran, Sudan and many other OIC countries have blasphemy laws, whether formal or informal. See, e.g., http://www.rationalistinternational.net/Shaikh/blasphemy_laws_in_pakistan.htm, accessed February 28, 2015.
[173] See http://www.forbes.com/2009/04/01/human-rights-council-opinions-columnists-united-nations.html, accessed February 28, 2015.
[174] In 2006, the US voted against the erection of the Human Rights Council, arguing that the rules to exclude human rights violators from being seated on the Council did not go far enough. See http://www.un.org/press/en/2006/ga10449.doc.htm, accessed November 25, 2014.

Last but not least, it is imperative that the U.S. government understand and acknowledge the full nature of the Global Jihad Movement and be able to define the threat. Though there's a military component, this war is primarily a war of ideas. The U.S. must be willing to name its enemy by name, take back its lexicon, and fight for its principles if America is to remain free.

AFTERWORD

When the Center for Security Policy's President, Frank Gaffney, Jr. tapped my shoulder inviting me to write a monograph on the OIC as part of CSP's Civilization Jihad Reader Series, I was thrilled.

As a 9/11 survivor, my original interest was in Islamic terrorism. But as time went on, I learned that the OIC and other Islamist groups were working fastidiously to silence all criticism of Islam and ultimately criminalize it. As difficult as this was to believe at first, years of extensive research revealed the truth about the OIC's supremacist aspirations. I studiously examined the OIC's UN Resolutions, Islamic blasphemy laws, additional Islamist efforts to protect Islam from "defamation", as well as the importance of free speech as a cornerstone freedom. I came to understand the critical role that free speech plays in protecting national security, religious freedom, and human rights. I gained a special awe for the uniqueness of the First Amendment as part and parcel of American exceptionalism.

Free speech in the West is increasingly under attack. It emanates from many quarters, but most significantly from Islamic supremacist groups and their enablers that protest "Islamophobic speech", whether it consists of gratuitous offense or truthful comments about Islamic terrorism and the nature of its ideological underpinnings.

Though there will always be people who insist on engaging in offensive expression, the right to do so must be protected. Otherwise, who will be the arbiter of what is or is not offensive? Should the expression of thoughts, emotions or opinions be criminalized? What about "offensive" facts?

The US Constitution holds no right to be free from insult. Nor should it. It is preferable to have ideas debated out in the open rather than pushed underground where secrecy imbues them with a power they might not otherwise have.

The Charlie Hebdo murders did not constitute an anomalous violent response to Islamic blasphemy. As delineated in the monograph, harsh penalties for insulting Islam are commonplace in the Muslim world. In the US, political correctness, multi-culturalism, and willful blindness of the facts are leading Americans down the road to self-censorship in accordance with Shariah blasphemy laws, seemingly unaware of the broader implications.

As this monograph was set to go to print, Pamela Geller and her colleague Robert Spencer, held a "Draw Muhammad Cartoon Contest" in Garland, Texas. While at a glance, this might have seemed offensive to most Muslims and even to many who are not Muslim, it must be understood that this event was held in *response* to the "Stand with the Prophet" conference, held after the Charlie Hebdo murders. That conference, at a minimum, championed enforcement of Islamic blasphemy laws and the silencing of speech offensive to Islam. At a maximum, presumably at least some in attendance supported (or at least refused to condemn) the murderous response to the Muhammad cartoon cover published by Charlie Hebdo. Clearly, they valued the implementation of Shariah blasphemy laws over the lives of those who violate them. This priority is demonstrated time and time again by the penalties meted out to those who blaspheme Islam, as well as by those who emphasize condemnation of satire and "Islamophobia" rather than the condemnation of its violent over-reactions.

It is imperative to note that Islam was not the only object of ridicule by Charlie Hebdo. Indeed, it was a satirical magazine, and over the years mocked many religions, prophets and public figures.

As I write this, tickets are being sold to a Broadway musical titled, "The Book of Mormon", the profanity of which is ultimate from a Mormon's point of view. Yet, the writers of that play, the same writers who edited out mockery of Muhammad from TV's "South Park" after receiving death threats, are in no fear of "violent extremist" Mormons. The "artists" of the "Piss Christ" and of the painting of the Virgin Mary with cow dung at the Brooklyn Museum, have not hired 24 hour security protection. Nor have churches started seminars at Ivy League universities to indoctrinate youth about the evils of "Christaphobia". Why is it only offense to Islam that draws such a violent response? The answer lies in the religion of Islam itself, which seeks to impose its supremacist ideals on both Muslims and infidels alike.

Pamela Geller's cartoon contest was a defiant insistence on the right to produce satire and mockery without exemptions for Islam. The winner, granted a prize of $12,500 was a former Muslim. Two Muslim gunmen, at least one of whom was ISIS inspired, came to the Curtis Culwell Center in body armor, carrying guns. They opened fire with the obvious intention to commit mass murder of the blasphemers inside the convention center. Though the event hosts had spent thousands on security, one security guard was shot and suffered a slight wound. The two gunmen were fatally shot by a Texas traffic officer.

Whether you supported Pamela Geller's contest on the merits of the issues, or whether you found it offensive, that she was able to hold such a contest legally without fear of criminal prosecution or being slapped with a fine, is a testament to the First Amendment's almost absolute right to free speech, which does not require a "balancing test" between freedom and offense as do the laws of most European countries.

True tolerance means putting up with an offensive joke, putting up with a cartoon or a movie or the expression of a viewpoint you dislike, in order to advance the greater cause of freedom. The events which transpired in Garland, Texas as this book was headed to print, and the implication that we should restrict speech in response, underscores the need for a greater appreciation of America's First Freedoms.

It is a sign of strength, not weakness, to be able to tolerate offense without overreaction. Appeasement to jihadists, whether stealth or violent, will only push us down a slippery slope toward dhimmitude and lead to freedom's eventual demise. For all those who hold America's cherished freedoms dear, let the tyranny of silence be no more.

APPENDIX 1: TEXT OF UNHRC RESOLUTION 10/22

As indicated in the footnotes, the wording of the Combating Defamation of Religions resolutions varied slightly from year to year. However, the basic concepts as analyzed in this monograph, remained the same. This text reflects Resolution 10/22 adopted by the UN Human Rights Council on March 26, 2009[175]:

---

[175] http://ap.ohchr.org/documents/E/HRC/resolutions/A_HRC_RES_10_22.pdf

Human Rights Council

Tenth Session

Resolution 10/22. Combating defamation of religions

The Human Rights Council,

Reaffirming the pledge made by all States under the Charter of the United Nations to promote and encourage universal respect for and observance of human rights and fundamental freedoms for all, without distinction as to race, sex, language or religion,

Reaffirming also that all human rights are universal, indivisible, interdependent and interrelated,

Recalling the 2005 World Summit Outcome adopted by the General Assembly in its resolution 60/1 of 16 September 2005, in which the Assembly emphasized the responsibilities of all States, in conformity with the Charter, to respect human rights and fundamental freedoms for all, without distinction of any kind, and acknowledged the importance of respect and understanding for religious and cultural diversity throughout the world,

Recognizing the valuable contribution of all religions to modern civilization and the contribution that dialogue among civilizations can make towards improved awareness and understanding of the common values shared by all humankind,

Welcoming the resolve expressed in the United Nations Millennium Declaration, adopted by the General Assembly on 8 September 2000, to take measures to eliminate the increasing acts of racism and xenophobia in many societies and to promote greater harmony and tolerance in all societies, and looking forward to its effective implementation at all levels,

Underlining in this regard the importance of the Durban Declaration and Programme of Action, adopted by the World Conference against Racism, Racial Discrimination, Xenophobia and Related Intolerance, held in Durban, South Africa, in 2001, welcoming the progress achieved in implementing them, and emphasizing that they constitute a solid foundation for the elimination of all scourges and manifestations of racism, racial discrimination, xenophobia and related intolerance,

Welcoming all international and regional initiatives to promote cross-cultural and interfaith harmony, including the Alliance of Civilizations and the International Dialogue on Interfaith Cooperation for Peace and Harmony, and their valuable efforts in the promotion of a culture of peace and dialogue at all levels,

Welcoming also the reports of the Special Rapporteur on contemporary forms of racism, racial discrimination, xenophobia and related intolerance submitted to the Council at its fourth, sixth and ninth sessions (A/HRC/4/19, A/HRC/6/6 and A/HRC/9/12), in which the Special Rapporteur highlighted the serious nature of the defamation of all religions and the need to complement legal strategies,

Noting with deep concern the instances of intolerance, discrimination and acts of violence against followers of certain faiths occurring in many parts of the world, in addition to the negative projection of certain religions in the media and the introduction and enforcement of laws and administrative measures that specifically discriminate against and target persons with certain ethnic and religious backgrounds, particularly Muslim minorities following the events of 11 September 2001, and that threaten to impede their full enjoyment of human rights and fundamental freedoms,

Stressing that defamation of religions is a serious affront to human dignity leading to a restriction on the freedom of religion of their adherents and incitement to religious hatred and violence,

Noting with concern that defamation of religions and incitement to religious hatred in general could lead to social disharmony and violations of human rights, and alarmed at the inaction of some States to combat this burgeoning trend and the resulting discriminatory practices against adherents of certain religions and, in this context, stressing the need to effectively combat defamation of all religions and incitement to religious hatred in general and against Islam and Muslims in particular,

Convinced that respect for cultural, ethnic, religious and linguistic diversity, as well as dialogue among and within civilizations, are essential for global peace and understanding, while manifestations of cultural and ethnic prejudice, religious intolerance and xenophobia generate hatred and violence among peoples and nations,

Underlining the important role of education in the promotion of tolerance, which involves acceptance by the public of and its respect for diversity,

Noting the various regional and national initiatives to combat religious and racial intolerance against specific groups and communities, and emphasizing, in this context, the need to adopt a comprehensive and non-discriminatory approach to ensure respect for all races and religions,

Recalling its resolution 7/19 of 27 March 2008 and General Assembly resolution 63/171 of 18 December 2008,

1. *Takes note* of the study of the United Nations High Commissioner for Human Rights on the compilation of existing legislation and jurisprudence concerning defamation of and contempt for religions (A/HRC/9/25) and the report of the Special Rapporteur on contemporary forms of racism, racial discrimination, xenophobia and related intolerance (A/HRC/9/12) presented to the Council at its ninth session;

2. *Expresses deep concern* at the negative stereotyping and defamation of religions and manifestations of intolerance and discrimination in matters of religion or belief still evident in the world, which have led to intolerance against the followers of these religions;

3. *Strongly deplores* all acts of psychological and physical violence and assaults, and incitement thereto, against persons on the basis of their religion or belief, and such acts directed against their businesses, properties, cultural centres and places of worship, as well as targeting of holy sites, religious symbols and venerated personalities of all religions;

4. *Expresses deep concern* at the continued serious instances of deliberate stereotyping of religions, their adherents and sacred persons in the media, as well as programmes and agendas pursued by extremist organizations and groups aimed at creating and perpetuating stereotypes about certain religions, in particular when condoned by Governments;

5. *Notes with deep concern* the intensification of the overall campaign of defamation of religions and incitement to religious hatred in general, including the ethnic and religious profiling of Muslim minorities in the aftermath of the tragic events of 11 September 2001;

6. *Recognizes* that, in the context of the fight against terrorism, defamation of religions and incitement to religious hatred in general have become aggravating factors that contribute to the denial of fundamental rights and freedoms of members of target groups, as well as to their economic and social exclusion;

7. *Expresses deep concern* in this respect that Islam is frequently and wrongly associated with human rights violations and terrorism and, in this regard, regrets the laws or administrative measures specifically designed to control and monitor Muslim minorities, thereby stigmatizing them and legitimizing the discrimination they experience;

8. *Reaffirms* the commitment of all States to the implementation, in an integrated manner, of the United Nations Global Counter-Terrorism Strategy, adopted without a vote by the General Assembly in its resolution 60/288 of 8 September 2006 and reaffirmed by the Assembly in its resolution 62/272 of 5 September 2008, in which it clearly reaffirms, inter alia, that terrorism cannot and should not be associated with any religion, nationality, civilization or group, as well as the need to reinforce the commitment of the international community to promote, among other things, a culture of peace and respect for all religions, beliefs and cultures and to prevent the defamation of religions;

9. *Deplores* the use of the print, audio-visual and electronic media, including the Internet, and any other means to incite acts of violence, xenophobia or related intolerance and discrimination against any religion, as well as the targeting of religious symbols and venerated persons;

10. *Emphasizes* that, as stipulated in international human rights law, including articles 19 and 29 of the Universal Declaration of Human Rights and articles 19 and 20 of the International Covenant on Civil and Political Rights, everyone has the right to hold opinions without interference and the right to freedom of expression, the exercise of which carries with it special duties and responsibilities and may therefore be subject to limitations only as provided for by law and are necessary for respect of the rights or reputations of others, protection of national security or of public order, public health or morals and general welfare;

11. *Reaffirms* that general comment No. 15 of the Committee on the Elimination of Racial Discrimination, in which the Committee stipulated that the prohibition of the dissemination of all ideas based upon racial superiority or hatred is compatible with freedom of opinion and expression, is equally applicable to the question of incitement to religious hatred;

12. *Strongly condemns* all manifestations and acts of racism, racial discrimination, xenophobia and related intolerance against national or ethnic, religious and linguistic minorities and migrants and the stereotypes often applied to them, including on the basis of religion or belief, and urges all States to apply and, where required, reinforce existing laws when such

xenophobic or intolerant acts, manifestations or expressions occur, in order to deny impunity for those who commit such acts;

13. *Urges* all States to provide, within their respective legal and constitutional systems, adequate protection against acts of hatred, discrimination, intimidation and coercion resulting from defamation of religions and incitement to religious hatred in general, and to take all possible measures to promote tolerance and respect for all religions and beliefs;

14. *Underscores* the need to combat defamation of religions and incitement to religious hatred in general by strategizing and harmonizing actions at the local, national, regional and international levels through education and awareness-building;

15. *Calls upon* all States to make the utmost effort, in accordance with their national legislation and in conformity with international human rights and humanitarian law, to ensure that religious places, sites, shrines and symbols are fully respected and protected, and to take additional measures in cases where they are vulnerable to desecration or destruction;

16. *Calls for* strengthened international efforts to foster a global dialogue for the promotion of a culture of tolerance and peace at all levels, based on respect for human rights and diversity of religions and beliefs, and urges States, non-governmental organizations, religious leaders as well as the print and electronic media to support and foster such a dialogue;

17. *Expresses its appreciation* to the High Commissioner for holding a seminar on freedom of expression and advocacy of religious hatred that constitutes incitement to discrimination, hostility or violence, in October 2008, and requests her to continue to build on this initiative, with a view to contributing concretely to the prevention and elimination of all such forms of incitement and the consequences of negative stereotyping of religions or beliefs, and their adherents, on the human rights of those individuals and their communities;

18. *Requests* the Special Rapporteur on contemporary forms of racism, racial discrimination, xenophobia and related intolerance to report on all manifestations of defamation of religions, and in particular on the serious implications of Islamophobia, on the enjoyment of all rights by their followers, to the Council at its twelfth session;

19. *Requests* the High Commissioner to report to the Council at its twelfth session on the implementation of the present resolution, including on the possible correlation between defamation of religions and the upsurge in incitement, intolerance and hatred in many parts of the world.

43rd meeting
26 March 2009

[Adopted by a recorded vote of 23 to 11, with 13 abstentions. The voting was as follows:

In favour: Angola, Azerbaijan, Bahrain, Bangladesh, Bolivia, Cameroon, China, Cuba, Djibouti, Egypt, Gabon, Indonesia, Jordan, Malaysia, Nicaragua, Nigeria, Pakistan, Philippines, Qatar, Russian Federation, Saudi Arabia, Senegal, South Africa;

Against: Canada, Chile, France, Germany, Italy, Netherlands, Slovakia, Slovenia, Switzerland, Ukraine, United Kingdom of Great Britain and Northern Ireland;

Abstaining: Argentina, Brazil, Bosnia and Herzegovina, Burkina Faso, Ghana, India, Japan, Madagascar, Mauritius, Mexico, Republic of Korea, Uruguay, Zambia.]

APPENDIX 2: TEXT OF UN RESOLUTION 16/18

Following is the text for UN Resolution 16/18 to Combat Intolerance Based on Religion or Belief. The Resolution was adopted in the Human Rights Council March 24, 2011[176]:

---

[176] http://www.refworld.org/pdfid/4db960f92.pdf

United Nations

A/HRC/RES/16/18

General Assembly

Distr.: General
12 April 2011

Original: English

Human Rights Council
Sixteenth session
Agenda item 9
Racism, racial discrimination, xenophobia and related
form of intolerance, follow-up and implementation
of the Durban Declaration and Programme of Action

Resolution adopted by the Human Rights Council*

16/18
Combating intolerance, negative stereotyping and stigmatization of, and discrimination, incitement to violence and violence against, persons based on religion or belief

The Human Rights Council,

Reaffirming the commitment made by all States under the Charter of the United Nations to promote and encourage universal respect for and observance of all human rights and fundamental freedoms without distinction as to, inter alia, religion or belief,

Reaffirming also the obligation of States to prohibit discrimination on the basis of religion or belief and to implement measures to guarantee the equal and effective protection of the law,

Reaffirming further that the International Covenant on Civil and Political Rights provides, inter alia, that everyone shall have the right to freedom of thought, conscience and religion or belief, which shall include freedom to have or to adopt a religion or belief of his choice, and freedom, either individually or in community with others and in public or private, to manifest his religion or belief in worship, observance, practice and teaching,

Reaffirming the positive role that the exercise of the right to freedom of opinion and expression and the full respect for the freedom to seek, receive and impart information can play in strengthening democracy and combating religious intolerance,

Deeply concerned about incidents of intolerance, discrimination and violence against persons based on their religion or belief in all regions of the world,

---

* The resolutions and decisions adopted by the Human Rights Council will be contained in the report of the Council on its sixteenth session (A/HRC/16/2), chap. I.

GE.11-12727

Deploring any advocacy of discrimination or violence on the basis of religion or belief,

Strongly deploring all acts of violence against persons on the basis of their religion or belief, as well as any such acts directed against their homes, businesses, properties, schools, cultural centres or places of worship,

Concerned about actions that wilfully exploit tensions or target individuals on the basis of their religion or belief,

Noting with deep concern the instances of intolerance, discrimination and acts of violence in many parts of the world, including cases motivated by discrimination against persons belonging to religious minorities, in addition to the negative projection of the followers of religions and the enforcement of measures that specifically discriminate against persons on the basis of religion or belief,

Recognizing the valuable contribution of people of all religions or beliefs to humanity and the contribution that dialogue among religious groups can make towards an improved awareness and understanding of the common values shared by all humankind,

Recognizing also that working together to enhance implementation of existing legal regimes that protect individuals against discrimination and hate crimes, increase interfaith and intercultural efforts, and to expand human rights education are important first steps in combating incidents of intolerance, discrimination and violence against individuals on the basis of religion or belief,

1. *Expresses deep concern* at the continued serious instances of derogatory stereotyping, negative profiling and stigmatization of persons based on their religion or belief, as well as programmes and agendas pursued by extremist organizations and groups aimed at creating and perpetuating negative stereotypes about religious groups, in particular when condoned by Governments;

2. *Expresses its concern* that incidents of religious intolerance, discrimination and related violence, as well as of negative stereotyping of individuals on the basis of religion or belief, continue to rise around the world, and condemns, in this context, any advocacy of religious hatred against individuals that constitutes incitement to discrimination, hostility or violence, and urges States to take effective measures, as set forth in the present resolution, consistent with their obligations under international human rights law, to address and combat such incidents;

3. *Condemns* any advocacy of religious hatred that constitutes incitement to discrimination, hostility or violence, whether it involves the use of print, audio-visual or electronic media or any other means;

4. *Recognizes* that the open public debate of ideas, as well as interfaith and intercultural dialogue, at the local, national and international levels can be among the best protections against religious intolerance and can play a positive role in strengthening democracy and combating religious hatred, and convinced that a continuing dialogue on these issues can help overcome existing misperceptions;

5. *Notes* the speech given by Secretary-General of the Organization of the Islamic Conference at the fifteenth session of the Human Rights Council, and draws on his call on States to take the following actions to foster a domestic environment of religious tolerance, peace and respect, by:

(*a*) Encouraging the creation of collaborative networks to build mutual understanding, promoting dialogue and inspiring constructive action towards shared policy goals and the pursuit of tangible outcomes, such as servicing projects in the fields of education, health, conflict prevention, employment, integration and media education;

(b) Creating an appropriate mechanism within Governments to, inter alia, identify and address potential areas of tension between members of different religious communities, and assisting with conflict prevention and mediation;

(c) Encouraging training of Government officials in effective outreach strategies;

(d) Encouraging the efforts of leaders to discuss within their communities the causes of discrimination, and evolving strategies to counter these causes;

(e) Speaking out against intolerance, including advocacy of religious hatred that constitutes incitement to discrimination, hostility or violence;

(f) Adopting measures to criminalize incitement to imminent violence based on religion or belief;

(g) Understanding the need to combat denigration and negative religious stereotyping of persons, as well as incitement to religious hatred, by strategizing and harmonizing actions at the local, national, regional and international levels through, inter alia, education and awareness-building;

(h) Recognizing that the open, constructive and respectful debate of ideas, as well as interfaith and intercultural dialogue at the local, national and international levels, can play a positive role in combating religious hatred, incitement and violence;

6. *Calls upon* all States:

(a) To take effective measures to ensure that public functionaries in the conduct of their public duties do not discriminate against an individual on the basis of religion or belief;

(b) To foster religious freedom and pluralism by promoting the ability of members of all religious communities to manifest their religion, and to contribute openly and on an equal footing to society;

(c) To encourage the representation and meaningful participation of individuals, irrespective of their religion, in all sectors of society;

(d) To make a strong effort to counter religious profiling, which is understood to be the invidious use of religion as a criterion in conducting questionings, searches and other law enforcement investigative procedures;

7. *Encourages* States to consider providing updates on efforts made in this regard as part of ongoing reporting to the Office of the United Nations High Commissioner for Human Rights;

8. *Calls upon* States to adopt measures and policies to promote the full respect for and protection of places of worship and religious sites, cemeteries and shrines, and to take measures in cases where they are vulnerable to vandalism or destruction;

9. *Calls for* strengthened international efforts to foster a global dialogue for the promotion of a culture of tolerance and peace at all levels, based on respect for human rights and diversity of religions and beliefs, and decides to convene a panel discussion on this issue at its seventeenth session, within existing resources.

46th meeting
24 March 2011
[Adopted without a vote.]

Made in the USA
Lexington, KY
22 August 2015